The Fellowship of Believers

Baptist Thought and Practice
Yesterday and Today

By
ERNEST A. PAYNE

General Secretary, Baptist Union of Great Britain and Ireland

With a Foreword by
Dr. H. WHEELER ROBINSON, M.A.

Enlarged Edition

THE CAREY KINGSGATE PRESS LTD.
6, Southampton Row, London, W.C.1

By the Same Author

*The Free Church Tradition in
the Life of England*

The Baptists of Berkshire

The Church Awakes

The Saktas (Religious Life of
India Series)

etc.

First Published, 1944
Enlarged Edition, 1952
Reprinted, 1954

Made and printed in Great Britain by
The Carey Kingsgate Press Ltd., 6, Southampton Row, London, W.C.1.

CONTENTS

AUTHOR'S NOTE

The first edition of this book, published in 1944, was undertaken at the request of the Publication Committee of the Baptist Union. I was under particular and deep obligation to the late Dr. Wheeler Robinson for counsel and encouragement in its preparation, for his reading of the typescript, and for his foreword. The typescript was also read by the present Principal of Regent's Park College, the Rev. R. L. Child, and to him I owe a debt of gratitude for many valuable suggestions. Much of the material was given at a Summer School for Baptist ministers of Northamptonshire and Huntingdonshire held in Oxford in July, 1944.

The call for a second edition has enabled me to make a few revisions, bringing certain passages up to date, and to include a number of other historical references. The subjects here treated have grown in interest and importance during recent years. I have added two entirely new chapters, those on Worship and Discipline, in an endeavour to present a more complete picture of Baptist polity and life, but the book remains only a brief introduction to themes which require much further thought and study if Baptists are to realise what is really involved in membership of the Body of Christ. There are two new appendices which will, I hope, prove useful for reference.

I repeat the words of Kierkegaard which I used as a motto to the first edition : "Life can only be understood backwards, but it must be lived forwards."

BAPTIST CHURCH HOUSE,   E.A.P.
LONDON, 1952.

FOREWORD

W H A T is the Church? Every form of it is compelled to give some sort of answer to that question, whether in theory or in practice, and that compulsion is felt today more than ever before. But you cannot answer the question, or even understand fully the answers given by others, unless you know two things. The first is what the Church *gives*. That means the inside knowledge of one who really shares in the intimate life of a community. To speak or write about the Church without ever knowing at first hand what it gives is like writing the geography of a land or the sociology of a people unvisited by the author. The Church creates a particular kind of life, for it is essentially the fellowship of men and women stirred to new life by a common faith. We must live in it and of it, in order to know what it is. The knowledge possessed in this way by many a quite ordinary man or woman with no gift of expression is worth far more than the opinion of some well-known journalist who shares the belief of Anatole France that the Church is like an old woman—alive, but only just!

The other essential for a worth-while answer to the question, What is the Church? is the ability to answer another question, What *was* the Church? History, true history, is not mere antiquarianism. It is the record of that life of yesterday which has made the life of today what it is. The present is always building on the past, and incorporating much more of it than we are apt to realize. If we are to plan and build wisely, we must know what those before us have done. What was the secret of those ancestors of ours which enabled them to pass on an inheritance to us? How often will the student of the past

6   FELLOWSHIP OF BELIEVERS

discover that what is acclaimed as the newly-found truth of today was already there through a succession of yesterdays!

This is one of the things in which Mr. Payne's little book is opportune and practical. He can teach his Baptist readers, for example, that their forerunners were in much closer association as Churches than they often are today. In some matters, the independence of the local Church is a valuable safeguard of Christian liberties. But it can easily become a form of selfishness alien to the Spirit of the Body of Christ, and far from the teaching and example of the New Testament. The early Separatists, from whom we Baptists emerged, were protesting against the parish as the basis of Church fellowship, because it included many who were not believers. But is there any reason why a particular group of *believers,* who happen to live in a particular geographical area, should necessarily be self-contained and self-sufficient, equipped with all the ministries and resources of the Church? In practice, we recognize that they are not, and we appoint area-super-intendents and committees and many other institutions to supplement the deficiencies of the local group. But it may well be that Baptists are now compelled to go deeper and to ask how far they are pledged to the policy of "Congregationalism." Is there any test of methods of organization and government save that they should be the best to promote the faith and service of the Gospel?

H. WHEELER ROBINSON.

Chapter One

THE SUBJECT AND THE SOURCES

I

"LET the Church be the Church." The slogan was coined in 1937 in connection with the Oxford Conference on Church, Community and State—one of the series of great Christian gatherings which future historians will note as taking place with increasing frequency in decades following the Edinburgh Missionary Conference of 1910. "Let the Church be the Church." The slogan has been echoed again and again during the past few years in many different parts of the world. But what is the Church, and where is it to be found? These questions have forced themselves forward with increasing frequency and insistence.

A variety of causes—chief among them a deepening realisation of the vastness of the task facing Christians in their attempt to evangelise the heathen world, a loss of confidence and power in Europe and North America, and a more vivid sense of the essentials of New Testament religion—has of recent decades brought closer together the different Christian groups into which the one Church split in the generations following the Reformation. Deeper unity and fellowship, closer co-operation and collaboration, have been sought in many parts of the world, and with no inconsiderable measure of success. In certain areas, as for example Canada and Scotland, and among certain groups springing not too distantly from a common source, such as the Methodists, important mergings and re-unitings have taken place. But as the main non-Roman Christian traditions have conferred together, they

have with increasing frequency found themselves held up
by awkward questions as to the Christian ministry and
the sacraments of Baptism and the Lord's Supper, questions about which their procedure differs, questions which
involve deeper issues regarding the nature of both the
Gospel itself and the Church. Again one asks, What is
the Church, and what is its relation to the Gospel?

The secular conflicts of recent decades have made the
question sound out still more insistently. On the Continent of Europe and in the Far East the followers of
Jesus Christ have found themselves facing demands by
the State which they were unwilling to concede. At first
the totalitarian and authoritarian powers merely restricted
the activities of Christians both within and without their
territories. Then more exacting demands were made.
In Nazi Germany there was an attempt at dictation
as to who should or should not be within the Christian
fellowship and as to how particular racial groups should
be treated. In spite of growing danger, many Christian
communities, Catholic, Orthodox and Protestant, with
mounting confidence, said No to these demands. The
stage seemed set for a renewed struggle between Church
and State, but one on a vaster scale than ever before.
This was indeed the background of the Oxford Conference of 1937, from which came the cry "Let the
Church be the Church." The World War which began
in 1939 broke in upon a situation already tense and confused in many lands. In Germany many courageous
Christian leaders continued to refuse unquestioning
obedience to the dictates of the State. In occupied lands
like Poland, Holland, Norway, Greece and even France,
the Church was the last stronghold of national resistance.
The same was true in the areas of South-East Asia and
the Pacific seized by the Japanese. More recently,
churches of various traditions have found themselves
face to face with régimes that are communist in sympathy

and character. The tensions which have resulted—in Asia as well as Europe—have been prolonged and complicated and have resulted in martyrdoms faced as heroically as any in Christian annals. The Church can never separate herself from the historical conflicts of the day, nor from the political, social and ideological influences which mould her members. It has, however, been made clear in the twentieth century, as in many earlier ages, that the Church in its various manifestations possesses inner resources against which even " the gates of hell " cannot prevail. What makes this body or institution so unexpectedly strong and resilient? A few years ago—as on a number of previous occasions—its early disappearance as an anachronism was confidently predicted. But there is clearly life still within it. What then is its nature and function?

The same question may be found agitating Christians concerned with the internal problems of their own particular fellowships. The Orthodox Church as a result of its experiences during the early years of the Russian Revolution, no less than the Lutheran and Reformed Churches in Germany, has had to busy itself with this fundamental issue. The Anglican Church, the Church of Scotland and the various Free Churches are all occupied with it. Problems of ecclesiastical adjustment and reorganisation all lead back to deeper questions about the Church itself. " There is great need today for laying fresh emphasis upon the doctrine of the Church." So declared the important report on *God's Will in Our Time,* presented to the General Assembly of the Church of Scotland in 1942 (p. 16). For seven years an influential group of Baptist ministers and laymen gave careful attention to practical matters connected with Baptist polity. At the last they were constrained to say : " As our work has proceeded we have reached the conclusion that the time has come for a fresh enquiry into the

Baptist doctrine of the Church. Not a few of our difficulties arise from an inadequate perception of the nature of the Church as the Body of Christ " (*Polity Report,* p. 5). Conclusions very similar have been reached by those in other Christian communions.

The matter has become more important and urgent since the founding, in 1948, of the World Council of Churches which binds together more than one hundred and fifty communions from more than forty lands. The World Council is not a new super-church directed on hierarchical and centralised lines, nor yet a loose-knit association held together by religious and social interests. It is a new phenomenon, and though it disavows the holding of an " ecclesiology " of its own, the secretary of the World Council, Dr. Visser 'tHooft, has claimed that it is " a body in which and through which, when it pleases God, a foretaste of the *una sancta* is given."

" Let the Church be the Church." Yes, but what is the Church, and what is its relation to the purpose of God? What is the right order of a Gospel Church? What place in its life have the sacraments? Are ministers or officers essential to its nature or well-being? What is the relation to one another of different Christian communions and of local Christian communities?

II

These are big questions. That they are being so widely asked after nearly two thousand years of Christian history suggests that there is no easy answer to them. Clearly, however, they are fundamental questions and those who busy themselves with them may hope for a reward.

To be again face to face with these issues represents a striking change from the situation a generation ago when many were ready to dissociate the idea of the Church from that of the Gospel and to reject the former as something added and unnecessary, indeed something that distorted the essential message of Jesus of Nazareth. Lecturing in Berlin in 1899, Harnack declared of Jesus : " He Himself founded no community in the sense of an organised union for divine worship " (*What is Christianity*? p. 152). In the same year A. M. Fairbairn announced : " There is no evidence that Jesus ever created, or thought of creating, an organised society. There is no idea He so little emphasises as the idea of the Church " (*Catholicism, Roman and Anglican*, p. 176). A few years later, T. R. Glover gave it as his opinion that Jesus " was not responsible either for the name or the idea of the church " (*The Conflict of Religions*, p. 157). As recently as 1920 A. S. Peake wrote : " It is a fact of immense importance and significance that Jesus Himself created no organisation " (*A Commentary on the Bible*, p. 645). It is only fair to note that these scholars were really protesting against particular types of Church and the theories and pretensions on which they were based. Nevertheless, their words may serve to remind us (1) that any enquiry about the nature of the Church has to be carried back to the New Testament itself, and (2) that we are moving out from a period of negation into one of renewed affirmation. The popular understanding, or misunderstanding, of what the scholars of a previous generation said has undoubtedly contributed to a carelessness in regard to the Church, both practical and theoretical. How far even Free Church scholars have moved from the days of Harnack and Fairbairn may be seen most conveniently in Dr. Newton Flew's *Jesus and His Church* (1938 ; 2nd edition, 1943) which argues that the idea of a new community, *ecclesia* or Church was fundamental to the teaching and intention of Jesus.[1]

[1] Cf. N. Micklem in *The Christian Faith*, 1944 edition, p. 111 : " If we eliminate the Church from the thought of our Lord, we throw away the one clue which interprets all He was and said and did." The whole chapter is a defence of this position.

In the chapters that follow we shall be concerned in particular with Baptist thought and practice regarding the Church, its ministry and its sacraments. Baptists already have a long and honourable history in many parts of the world. The name by which they are known fastens upon their attitude to one of the two Gospel sacraments. Like many other nicknames, it may both within and without the ranks of the Baptists distract attention from more important matters.[2] It has indeed been seriously claimed for Baptists by their most distinguished modern historian that "their distinctive feature is the doctrine of the Church" (Whitley, *A History of British Baptists,* p. 4). If this is so, then they are likely to have an important contribution to make to the modern debate, and it is very desirable that their views be clearly set forth. Their own house has to be set in order. Baptists have probably suffered as much as any Christian community of recent years from the general slackness, casualness and confusion regarding the doctrine of the Church, and have departed as widely as any from the traditions of their fathers. If they are to make their contribution to the modern discussion of these questions and to meet the challenge of the modern situation, one of their first tasks is to rediscover what have been the essential and characteristic notes of their witness.

This is not as easy as might be expected. Baptists have produced no very learned array of theologians, and those who have been outstanding among them have not given a great deal of attention to the doctrine of the Church. The materials for a study of Baptist thought and practice—and it is with the English tradition that we shall be mainly concerned[3]—have been by no means ex-

[2] Note that in its original form, "Anabaptist," it was repudiated by the seventeenth century pioneers. See p. 72 below.
[3] For American thought and practice see E. T. Hiscox, *Baptist Church Directory,* 1859 and W. R. McNutt, *Polity and Practice in Baptist Churches,* 1935.

haustively worked over. They may be conveniently divided into five categories : (1) certain pronouncements issued in recent years by the Council of the Baptist Union of Great Britain and Ireland (and by one or two other organised Baptist bodies), mainly in reply to questions or proposals from the Conferences on Faith and Order held at Lausanne in 1927 and Edinburgh in 1937, or in preparation for that at Lund in 1952; (2) the small number of treatises directly devoted to questions of the Church by Baptist writers, the most notable of which seem to be Daniel Turner's *Compendium of Social Religion* (1758 : 2nd edition, 1778), the relevant sections of John Gill's *Body of Practical Divinity* (1770), Charles Stovel's *Hints on the Regulation of Christian Churches* (1835), Joseph Angus's prize essays *The Voluntary System* (1839) and *Christian Churches* (1862), Dawson Burns's *Manual of the Christian Principles and Church Polity of the General Baptists of the New Connexion* (1863) and, of recent days, the provocative but not very happily named booklet by Dr. Dakin, *The Baptist View of the Church and Ministry* (1944) and the volume by R. C. Walton entitled, *The Gathered Community* (1946) ;[4] (3) the Circular Letters of the various Baptist Associations, particularly those of the closing decades of the eighteenth century—which usually dealt with theological and ecclesiastical topics and therefore form a most important, but so far largely unregarded, field for the study of Baptist life and faith; (4) the reports on Baptist procedure which may be found in Church and Association Minute Books, Rippon's *Baptist Register* (1790-1802), and the Baptist magazines and periodicals which have succeeded it; and (5) the early Baptist Confessions,

[4] To these should perhaps be added John Smyth's *Principles and Inferences Concerning the Visible Church*, 1607, and *The Differences of the Churches of the Separation*, 1608, but both these important pamphlets were written before he had come to " Baptist " views.

mainly from the seventeenth century—a convenient though not wholly adequate collection of which may be found in W. J. McGlothlin's *Baptist Confessions of Faith* (1910).

The first of these categories—obviously the most easily accessible—is not as fruitful as might be expected. The Baptist reply to the (Lambeth) Appeal to all Christian People, adopted by the Annual Assembly at Leeds in 1926, is a very valuable statement,[5] including important sections dealing with the Church, Ministry and Sacraments, but it is brief and does not seem to have been based on a great deal of historical study. Nor does it deal with many of the questions that are now seen to be important from the standpoint of Baptist polity as well as that of our relations with other groups of Christians. The comments passed by the Baptist Union Council in 1930 on the official report of the Lausanne Conference (at which, unfortunately, Baptists were not officially represented) were in the main scrappy and negative. They will be found together with a number of general Free Church statements, in the drawing up of which individual Baptists had a share, in *Convictions*, edited by L. Hodgson (S.C.M. Press, 1934). The Theological Commission appointed by the Lausanne Conference to carry further the discussion of certain of the issues raised brought together a number of important papers in the volume *The Ministry and the Sacraments* (ed. by Dunkerley, 1937). There are two brief Baptist contributions, the one by Professor I. G. Matthews, of Crozer Seminary, U.S.A., which adopts a largely " Zwinglian " view of the sacraments, and one by Dr. A. C. Underwood, of Rawdon College, protesting against the inadequacy of this view and stating his readiness to accept Dr. J. S. Whale's exposition of the Congregationalist position, save as regards the subject of baptism. In 1932 the Baptist Union Council set up a special committee on the question

[5] See Appendix B.

of union between Baptists, Congregationalists and Presbyterians. Its report, issued in 1937, is an important document, but it concentrates almost exclusively upon baptism and has little to say directly about the nature of the Church, or its organization and ministry. The same must be said of the report of a Commission on " The Baptist Contribution to Christian Unity," appointed by the Baptist World Alliance, which was considered at the Baptist World Congress in Atlanta in 1939. The statement " The Doctrine of the Church," approved by the Baptist Union Council in March 1948, represents the first theological declaration made by British Baptists in modern times.[6]

It would appear, therefore, that the fresh enquiry into the Baptist doctrine of the Church for which the Polity Commission asked is from every point of view overdue and that it is likely to be a substantial task demanding a knowledge of Baptist history and a grasp of essential Baptist principles and inevitably leading back to the New Testament itself. The pages that follow are intended as no more than a preliminary submission of some of the historical evidence that has to be considered and some suggestions as to its bearing on modern issues. Theology and doctrine, particularly Christian theology and doctrine, must never be divorced from history, and, as has been well said, " history should be studied always as a process ; not as a picture."

III

There are one or two further preliminary considerations which must be kept constantly in mind. Firstly, Baptists come of Reformation stock. Their teaching and practice cannot be separated from that of other Reformation

[6] See Appendix D.

bodies. In some periods Baptists have given little direct attention to questions of Church and Ministry, because they have been quite content to accept what others have had to say on these matters. A book like John Owen's *The True Nature of a Gospel Church* (1689) undoubtedly exercised a wide influence on Baptists, though, as we shall suggest later, it does not adequately represent the position of many of them on certain important matters. In the closing decades of the nineteenth century most Baptists accepted the views put forward by Dr. R. W. Dale in his *Manual of Congregational Principles* (1884).

Secondly, Baptists come of no one Reformation stream exclusively. Many of them have been very strongly Calvinistic in their theology. It would even be urged by some today that no other Christian body remains so loyally Calvinistic in essential belief as does the Baptist. Nevertheless, those who know their Baptist history are never likely to echo the cry that has been heard within Congregationalism of recent years : " We are of Geneva." Baptists have never looked exclusively to one city, even to Geneva, for the inspiration of their thought and practice. The possible connection between the early English Baptists and the Continental Anabaptists is an intricate and thorny historical problem.[7] Now that the term "Anabaptist" is seen to have been as wildly hurled about and to have had as little definite content as the modern "Bolshevik",[8] when used as a general term of abuse, there is less reason for indignantly repudiating it than there was. The Anabaptist movement was one of the most significant and vital religious movements of the

[7] See, e.g. *Baptist Quarterly*, II, pp. 24f., papers by W. T. Whitley and A. J. D. Farrer; *Transactions of the Congregational Historical Society*, XII and XIII, articles by Duncan B. Heriot. Cf. E. A. Payne *The Anabaptists of the 16th Century*, 1949.

[8] This is admitted by the distinguished Roman Catholic historian, Maximin Piette. See *John Wesley in the Evolution of Protestantism*, 1938, p. 36.

Reformation epoch and those who think of it solely or mainly in terms of the unfortunate and disgraceful happenings during the siege of Münster are sadly astray. Some Anabaptist influence, direct and indirect, almost certainly went to the making of the earliest Baptist communities in this country and there is every reason to be proud of it. Mennonite influence there certainly was during the years when Baptist thought and practice was in its embryonic stage among Separatist exiles in Holland. It is, therefore, to be noted that, while Luther's theological concern centred around *sola fide,* and Calvin's around the sovereignty and will of God, that of the Anabaptists and Mennonites centred in the New Testament *ecclesia,* not, as some have urged, in individual piety. The earliest "General " Baptists are perhaps better described as pre-Calvinist than as anti-Calvinist in their theology. Their practice in Church matters, as we shall see, was markedly different from that of the earliest Separatists and Congregationalists. From the beginning of the seventeenth century to the end of the nineteenth, Baptist life ran in two distinct streams—that of the General Baptists and that of the Particular or Calvinistic Baptists. There were differences between them of practice as well as doctrine. This is one of the reasons why it is difficult as well as dangerous to generalise or dogmatise about Baptist beliefs. There has been variety in our life, and sometimes tension. Things stressed in one generation have sometimes fallen into the background in the next, only to be revived again later on. It is a rich and diverse tradition to which we are able to appeal. For this inheritance Baptists may well be grateful, though the more they have made it their own, the more they will realise how careful they must be not to use the adjective " Baptist " in any narrow or exclusive sense.

Thirdly, Baptists come of the lineage of John Smyth, who in 1606 drew up the historic covenant of the

Separatist church in and around Gainsborough. "As the Lord's free people," said William Bradford, who was one of the company, and who later went with the Pilgrim Fathers to America " (they) joined themselves by a covenant of the Lord into a church estate, in the fellowship of the Gospel, to walk in all His ways, made known, or to be made known unto them, according to their best endeavours, whatsoever it should cost them, the Lord assisting them." The temper and outlook of these words were no doubt the inspiration of the better known dictum of John Robinson, a slightly younger man, deeply influenced by Smyth : " The Lord has more Truth yet to break forth out of His Word." Smyth sent his friends and associates upon a quest and a pilgrimage. Theirs was, by its very nature, a progressive covenant. With the New Testament in their hands, they were to promise to conform to what should be made known to them by the Spirit. Loyalty to this led in Smyth's own case to his becoming convinced that admission into the true Church should be by baptism in the scriptural manner. Later, doubting the rightness of the self-baptism with which he had begun the reconstitution of his church, he joined himself with many of his followers to the Mennonites, among whom, he felt, the truly scriptural usage had been maintained; though this action meant that the partnership between himself and his friend, Helwys, was broken. When, in 1612, in the last months of his life, Smyth wrote his *Retraction and Confirmation,* he had moved a stage farther and had come to feel that "matters of the outward Church and Ceremonies" were of secondary importance to Christian charity. "Difference in Judgment for matter of circumstance," he declared, "as are all things of the outward church, shall not cause me to refuse the brotherhood of any penitent and faithful Christian whatsoever" (*Works,* ed. by Whitley, II, p. 755).

The principle of the Gainsborough covenant is of fundamental importance for an understanding of Baptist life at its best. Baptists have claimed freedom from the authority of any sacerdotal hierarchy, freedom from the State, freedom of conscience, freedom of private judgment. They have been, on the whole consistently, suspicious of creeds and verbal statements. Hence, in large measure, the difficulty of tying them down at any point to belief in this or that theory. They have claimed the guidance of the living Spirit of Christ present within His Church, a guidance inspired, confirmed and held in check by appeal to the Scriptures and, in particular, to those of the New Testament. The final court of appeal has been neither to church pronouncements, nor to history and tradition as such, but to the conscience of the church inspired by the Spirit of God as a result of the study of the Bible. " The deepest impulse of Baptist life has been the upholding of the sole and exclusive authority of Jesus Christ against all possible encroachment," said Dr. John Clifford at the Baptist World Congress of 1911. That has implied the Lordship of Christ within the Church— the Lordship of the living Christ still guiding and directing His people.

These things should be kept carefully in mind in considering the evidence as to Baptist belief and practice which will be set forth.

Chapter Two

THE VISIBLE CHURCH

I

BAPTISTS are among the children of the Reformation. They came of that mighty movement which sought to restore the purity of the Church. The corruptions of medieval Catholicism had become so great that over wide areas of Europe there was swift response to the trumpet call of Luther and his associates. With enthusiasm and zeal men set about sweeping away a system which had come to hinder rather than help their approach to God. The original Lutheran movement was primarily religious. Its emphasis was upon personal justification by faith and the right of private judgment in matters of religion. The word uttered by Luther was of epoch-making significance, a rediscovery of vast resources of spiritual power, which had revolutionary consequences for every side of European life. It is well, however, to remember that " it had never been Luther's aim either to found a new Church, or even within the historically existing Church to carry out any elaborately pre-arranged form of reorganisation " (H. E. Jacobs, *E.R.E.*, VIII, p. 202). He was himself never quite at ease in the discussions regarding the form of Church order which was to follow from the principles which he had enunciated. Only slowly did the full consequence of his appeal to Scripture become apparent. The varied views which were soon to be found among the Reformers showed the complexity of the issues involved. Before long Zwinglians, Anabaptists and Calvinists were all busy with the task of trying to erect a Church order which should be in accordance with that portrayed in the New Testament. That they differed on many matters is not surprising when one considers the newness of the quest upon which they were engaged, the confused political situation of the time, the verbal authority they ascribed to the text of Scripture and the nature of the evidence with which they had to deal.

The new ideas were soon at work like a ferment in England. Henry VIII, the great Tudor sovereign, was at first a vigorous and honoured champion of the old Catholicism against the subversive views of Luther. Later, personal and political considerations led him to break with Rome, and he found certain of the principles enunciated by the Reformers not inconvenient to him. The English Reformation was, however, essentially a compromise, an attempt to go so far but no farther, an effort to set up a National Church with the supreme authority firmly in the hands of the sovereign and the bishops instead of those of the Pope. There was soon a strong Puritan party convinced that the reform of the English Church ought to be more radical, far more like that which had been carried through on the Continent, particularly in those areas which had adopted the views of Calvin.

From among the Puritans came the Separatists. Those who despaired of any adequate reform of the ecclesiastical abuses in this country and those who, in their study of Scripture, found themselves led to reject altogether a State-established Church and a Church governed from above by an episcopally ordained hierarchy, or even by synods of presbyters, formed "Separatist" Churches, local communities of believers in the Gospel starting *de novo* to model their life and worship on the New Testament. Persecution by the civil and religious authorities drove many of the Separatists abroad, first to Holland, later to the American Colonies. From among the

Separatists came the Baptists. A New Testament Church, they said, must surely observe the New Testament rites in a New Testament manner. They were but one among many groups who in the opening decades of the seventeenth century earnestly sought to discover the pattern of Gospel churchmanship. Underlying the bitter theological controversies and the political upheavals of Stuart and Commonwealth England there was a wistful searching for the true Church. We who, three centuries later, are vexed with many of the same problems, should have a new sympathy with our spiritual ancestors.

Certain fairly clear convictions emerged during the course of the Reformation movement which has been cursorily outlined in the preceding paragraphs. They are part of the religious heritage of those whose beliefs about the Church we shall examine more closely. The Continental Reformers—Lutheran, Anabaptist and Calvinist—the Puritans, the Separatists and their seventeenth century descendants, all held firmly to the principle that salvation is by faith, that is, by direct individual response to the grace offered by God in Christ. Neither priest nor Church stands between God and the believer. Secondly, all alike made an appeal to Scripture and regarded it as authoritative for faith and also, to a greater or lesser extent, for practice. In *The Problem of Authority in the Continental Reformers* (1946), Mr. Rupert Davies has studied the somewhat different attitudes to Scripture taken by Luther, Zwingli and Calvin. The Anabaptists and Spiritualists had also their own approach. But all turned to the Bible for guidance in their church polity. It was perhaps almost inevitable that, thirdly, in reaction from the idea of the Church as a great visible institution centralised and authoritarian, not a few should stress the idea of the Church invisible, the company of the elect whose names are known only to God, and that they should place their emphasis—so far as the Church visible is

concerned—on the local company of believers, who because of their common faith come together deliberately
to carry out the ordinances of the Gospel and who can
rely on the word of Jesus recorded in Matthew xviii. 20 :
" Where two or three are gathered in My name, there am
I in the midst of them." These three ideas—worked out
in varied fashion—are the foundations of the tradition
in which Baptists stand. They form the background of
the seventeenth century creeds and confessions to which
we now turn. They have remained basic to our life and
witness down to the present time.

There is, however, a fourth determining principle, of
equal importance, to which we have already called
attention, viz. a belief in the presence of the Spirit of
the living Christ with His people, leading them on to an
ever fuller apprehension of truth and to an ever holier
way of life. The Separatists and their descendants were
avowed " seekers." They recognised themselves as
voyaging on largely uncharted seas. They were sure,
however, that, if they were faithful, the way would be
revealed to them.

II

With these things in mind we may turn to some of the
early Baptist statements regarding the Church and to a
consideration of the church polity which they set forth.
We may well begin with some sentences from the final
Confession of the company to whom John Smyth minis-
tered in Holland. Smyth is generally regarded as the
father of the General Baptists, that is, the earlier of the
two main streams of Baptist witness. The opening
articles of the Confession set out at length, in the
language of Scripture, a theological compendium, leading
up to an emphatic declaration of the necessity of personal
repentance and faith. It continues :

" 62. That as Christ who was above the law notwithstanding was made under the law, for our cause : so the regenerate in love to others, can and will do no other, than use the outward things of the church, for the gaining and support of others : and so the outward church and ordinances are always necessary, for all sorts of persons whatsoever.

" 64   That the outward church visible consists of penitent persons only, and of such as believing in Christ bring forth fruits worthy amendment of life.

" 65.   That the visible church is a mystical figure outwardly, of the true, spiritual invisible church; which consisteth of the spirits of just and perfect men only, that is, of the regenerate. . . .

" 69. That all penitent and faithful Christians are brethren in the communion of the outward church, wheresoever they live, by what name soever they are known, which in truth and zeal, follow repentance and faith, though compassed with never so many ignorances and infirmities; and we salute them all with a holy kiss, being heartily grieved that we which follow after one faith, and one spirit, one Lord, and one God, one body, and one baptism, should be rent into so many sects and schisms : and that only for matters of less moment " (McGlothlin, op. cit., pp. 78-9).[1]

A noble spirit breathes through this last clause and the words deserve to be far better known than they are. They show a breadth and charity which, while they have not

[1] Of the hundred clauses of the Confession only three are without Scripture references. This is one of the three. But Whitley, *The Works of John Smyth*, 1915, I, p. lxxi, seems hardly to do Smyth justice when he says : " The question never became important to Smyth how one church was related to another, so he never raised it, much less examined Scripture to answer it. He neither affirmed nor denied Independency."

always been universally echoed among Baptists, have yet happily never been without witnesses in their midst. It is only after this clause, which has important implications for the doctrine of the visible church, that Smyth goes on to define the baptism of penitent and faithful persons, the Lord's Supper, the ministry of the church, Christian discipline, freedom of conscience, Christian ethics and finally the Christian hope, as he and his friends viewed these things.

The Confession of the group who followed Thomas Helwys and returned to London with him in 1612, there establishing the first Baptist church in England, is shorter than that of Smyth but more explicit regarding the church.

" 10. That the Church of Christ is a company of faithful people, separated from the world by the word and Spirit of God, being knit unto the Lord, and one unto another, by baptism, upon their own confession of the faith and sins.

" 11. That though, in respect of Christ, the Church be one, yet it consisteth of divers particular congregations, even so many as there shall be in the world, every of which congregation, though they be but two or three, have Christ given them, with all the means of their salvation, are the Body of Christ, and a whole Church. And therefore may, and ought, when they are come together to pray, prophesy and break bread, and administer in all the holy ordinances, although as yet they have no officers, or that their officers should be in prison, sick, or by any other means hindered from the church.

" 12. That as one congregation hath Christ, so hath all, and that the Word of God cometh not out from any one, neither to any one congregation in particular, but unto every particular church, as it doth unto all the world, and therefore no church ought to challenge any prerogative over any other. . . .

" 16.   That the members of every church or congregation ought to know one another, that so they may perform all the duties of love one towards another both to soul and body . . . ." (McGlothlin, pp. 88-90, spelling modernised and Scripture references omitted).

Here the spiritual autonomy of each local company of believers is asserted, their right to appoint their own officers claimed, and their numbers limited to a group who can have " particular knowledge one of another." Helwys defended the right of the congregation to observe the Lord's Supper even when it had no ordained pastor or he was in prison.   Other groups of Baptists as we shall see, scrupled to do this, as did most other Separatists.

In practice it was some time before Baptists established very large churches.   In the case of the General Baptists these usually covered a considerable geographical area, divided for convenience into a number of worshipping centres.   Only occasionally could the members all meet together for the Lord's Supper or for church business. The scattered community was held together by its officers, some of whom had to travel long distances.   At the end of the seventeenth century there was, for example, a London church functioning as one unit for the election of elders and deacons which had at least seven sections in different parts of the metropolis.[2]   Similarly, at Slapton in Northamptonhire might be found a church with members in nine or ten different villages and a presiding elder living fifteen miles away in Northampton.[3]

[2] See *Baptist Quarterly*, VII, pp. 321f.
[3] See Anderson, *The Baptist Churches at Weston by Weedon, etc.,* 1930.

These early Baptists jealously guarded the right of the local church to appoint its own officers, and specifically rejected any suggestion that one church could have authority over another. They suffered persecution for their resistance to the attempts of the magistrates and the bishops of the Established Church to control them. They were never, however, so foolish as to believe that a particular church did not need the fellowship of other churches. Representatives of thirty congregations in Leicestershire, Lincolnshire and adjoining counties met in 1651 and drew up a common Confession to which they invited the adherence of other churches " in England, Wales, Army, or elsewhere." Nine years later, representatives of General Baptist churches all over the kingdom met in London and drew up what is usually called " the Standard Confession of 1660."

Eighteen years later, in what is known as the " Orthodox Creed " of 1678, drawn up by General Baptists from Buckinghamshire, Oxfordshire and adjoining counties, " General Councils, or Assemblies " were thus provided for and described :

" XXXIX. General councils, or assemblies, consisting of Bishops, Elders, and Brethren, of the several churches of Christ, and being legally convened, and met together out of all the churches, and the churches appearing there by their representatives, make but one church, and have lawful right, and suffrage in this general meeting, or assembly, to act in the name of Christ; it being of divine authority, and is the best means under heaven to preserve unity, to prevent heresy, and superintendency among or in any congregation whatsoever within its own limits, or jurisdiction. And to such a meeting, or assembly, appeals ought to be made, in case any injustice be done, or heresy, and schism countenanced, in any

particular congregation of Christ, and the decisive
voice in such general assemblies is the major part,
and such general assemblies have lawful power
to hear, and determine, as also to excommunicate "
(McGlothlin, p. 154).

The words "make but one church" are particularly
significant. The General Baptists were clearly not independents in the commonly accepted use of the term. It is
worth noting, moreover, that the Confession is supported
at this point by references to the Council at Jerusalem
recorded in Acts xv., to Matthew xviii. 18-20, and to
1 Corinthians v. 4-6. In 1696 a General Assembly of
General Baptist " messengers " declared that independence
is " very dangerous and detrimental." [4]

Similarly, the Particular Baptists, a Calvinistic group
who came out of Separatism and Congregationalism on
the issue of believers' baptism, and who spread rapidly
during the Commonwealth period, established " Associations " of churches which drew up common confessions.
A Confession first produced by seven London congregations in 1644, and several times re-issued with larger
numbers adhering to it, has been described by McGlothlin
as " perhaps the most independent of the Baptist Confessions and . . . one of the noblest productions ever put
forth by them " (*op. cit.*, p. 170). He claims that it
probably still represents the view of the Baptists of the
world more nearly than any other single Confession. In
it there occurs this article :

"XLVII. And although the particular Congregations be distinct and severall Bodies, every one a
compact and knit Citie in it selfe; yet are they all to
walk by one and the same Rule, and by all meanes
convenient to have the counsell and help one of an-

[4] W. T. Whitley, *Minutes of the General Assembly, I*, p. 42.

other in all needfull affaires of the Church, as members of one body in the common faith under Christ their onely head " (*op. cit.*, p. 186-7).

Almost all subsequent Particular Baptist Confessions show the strong influence of the historic Confession laid before Parliament by the Westminster divines in 1646 and generally accepted as a classic exposition of Calvinism.[5] Save in regard to the spiritual autonomy of the local congregation in the appointment of its own officers and on the matter of believers' baptism, the Baptist variations are mainly verbal.

All these documents are inspired by what may rightly be described as High Churchmanship. A particular group of believers is conceived as drawn together into fellowship and by the selection of officers, the proper observance of the sacraments and the disciplining of its members may be assured of the presence of Christ and may claim to be truly part of the visible Church. But it must be in communion with other local churches. That is an essential part of its churchmanship. The individual groups are regarded as " separate hearts of one whole " —to borrow the language of a modern poet.[6] The 1677 Particular Baptist Confession (reaffirmed in 1689 after the accession of William and Mary by the representatives of one hundred and seven churches in England and Wales, and subsequently issued in

[5] It was issued in 1648 in English and Latin by Parliamentary authority and was until the Restoration the Confessional Standard of the United Kingdom.

[6] Laurence Housman, *The Continuing City*. Cf. P. T. Forsyth's metaphor of the local church as an " outcrop " of the total and continuous church, one everywhere (see *The Church and the Sacraments*, 1917). Cf. also A. G. Hebert, *The Form of the Church*, 1944, p. 64, on " the partial truth of the Congregationalist conception of the Church, in which it has been truly seen that the whole mystery of the Church is present in each local part,"

many different editions)[7] makes this quite explicit.

> " Chap. XXVI. 14. As each Church and all the
> members of it are bound to pray continually for the
> good and prosperity of all the Churches of Christ, in
> all places; and upon all occasions to further it (every
> one within the bounds of their places and callings in
> the exercise of their gifts and graces) so the
> Churches (when planted by the providence of God
> so as they may enjoy opportunity and advantage for
> it) ought to hold communion amongst themselves for
> their peace, increase of love and mutual edification "
> (McGlothlin, p. 267-8).

Questions of doctrine and administration, and even of
the internal peace of individual churches, should be submitted to the representatives of churches meeting in
assembly. Their conclusions cannot be imposed upon the
particular churches, or their officers. An assembly had
not for the Particular Baptists what is called " church-
power." The acceptance of decisions must be voluntary.
Nevertheless, in practice the spiritual authority of such
assemblies was very great, and they were an essential part
of the churchmanship of the early Baptists. This is
being increasingly recognised by historians. Writing of
Wales, Dr. Thomas Richards has said : " The nearest
approach to Presbyterianism . . . was the close organisation of the Particular Baptists in the South." Dr.

[7] McGlothlin, p. 219, describes it as "the most influential and
important of all Baptist Confessions." The sections bearing on
the matters discussed in this book will be found in Appendix A.
In a review of the first edition of this book the late Dr. A. C.
Underwood urged the unwary reader to remember that the Confessions of 1644 and 1677 derived their influence from the sections
dealing with baptism and typical Calvinistic doctrines rather than
those dealing with the Church and Ministry, pointing out that
subscription to the 1677 Confession is now required only by
Gospel Standard Strict Baptists who have remained rigidly
Calvinistic in doctrine and are in organisation the most atomistic
of all Baptist groups.

Duncan Coomer goes farther. "From the beginning," he says, with England in mind, "the Baptists were far more inclined to united action than either of the other two denominations," that is, the Presbyterians and the Independents.[8]

III

This matter is of considerable importance. Associations, Synods, Unions and Assemblies of churches are not to be regarded as optional and secondary. They are the necessary expression of Christian fellowship, a necessary manifestation of the Church visible. The local congregation is not truly a church if it lives an entirely separate life. We have already referred to the influence of John Owen's *True Nature of a Gospel Church* in Baptist circles. The great Independent divine there sets out, in language which Baptists often borrowed, the principles of Congregationalism. It is right that Baptists as well as Congregationalists should have their attention called to the important part which Owen assigned to fellowship and communion between churches.[9]

Churches, said Owen, once they have been properly constituted, " are obliged into mutual Communion among themselves, which is their consent, endeavour and conjunction in and for the promotion of the Edification of

[8] T. Richards, *The Puritan Movement in Wales,* 1920, p. 202; D. Coomer, *English Dissent,* 1947, p. 59.

[9] For the discussion of this issue by Congregationalists see D. T. Jenkins, *The Nature of Catholicity,* 1942, and N. Micklem, *Congregationalism and the Church Catholic,* 1943. It should be noted how much more positive is this section of Owen's work than the corresponding section in Thomas Hooker, *A Survey of the Summe of Church Discipline,* 1648, which describes conditions in New England and was long influential on the Congregationalism of the United States. cf. *The Cambridge Platform,* 1648.

the Catholic Church, and therein their own, as they are Parts and Members of it " (*op. cit.*, 1689 edition, p. 234). He urged the widest possible co-operation and fellowship between Christians who have all " one and the same God and Father, one Lord Jesus Christ, one Faith and one Doctrine of Faith, one hope of their calling or the promised Inheritance, one Regeneration, one Baptism, one Bread and Wine; united into God and Christ in one Spirit, through the bond of Faith and Love " (p. 242). He defined their communion with one another as " their joint actings in the same Gospel Duties towards God in Christ, with their mutual actings towards each other, with respect unto the end of their Institution and Being, which is the glory of Christ in the Edification of the whole Catholick Church " (p. 244). " No Church therefore is so Independent, as that it can always, and in all Cases, observe the Duties it owes unto the Lord Christ and the Church Catholick, by all those Powers which it is able to act in itself distinctly, without conjunction with others. And the Church that confines its Duty unto the Acts of its own Assemblies, cuts itself off from the external Communion of the Church Catholick; nor will it be safe for any Man to commit the Conduct of his Soul to such a Church " (p. 251).

These are searching and weighty words, strikingly relevant to our modern situation. What follows is even more pointed. " That particular Church which extends not its Duty beyond its own Assemblies and Members, is fallen off from the principal end of its Institution. And every Principle, Opinion, or Persuasion, that inclines any Church to confine its Care and Duty unto its own Edification only; yea, or of those only which agree with it in some peculiar practice, making it neglective of all due means of the Edification of the Church Catholick, is Schismatical " (p. 251).

Owen believed that it was by means of synods and

councils that the churches should express their fellowship in the Church Catholick. These synods should consider questions of faith and order, questions of peace and unity, questions of discipline (i.e. Christian ethics), questions of worship. They have the duty and responsibility of positive action on these matters and have not to wait until specifically appealed to. Owen expressly provided, however, that even an individual, being " not only a Member of (a) particular Church, but by virtue thereof of the Catholick Church also " (p. 252), had the right of appeal to a synod. He ascribed to synods a three-fold power : (1) declarative; (2) constitutive; and (3) executive— the last in cases of jurisdiction submitted to it.

In these concluding and largely neglected pages of Owen's treatise is to be found a comprehensive justification, on Congregationalist principles, of the movement towards co-operation and union among those of different Christian traditions which has occupied so much of the energy of Christian leaders during the past thirty years. There is also to be found the theological and biblical rationale of unions and associations of churches sharing a common practice and organisation.

IV

Whilst they have often shown themselves somewhat shy of the wider implications of Owen's contentions, Baptists have been notable from the earliest times for the vigour of their Association life.[10] We have already noted the explicit provision for this in the seventeenth century Confessions. It has continued a vital part of Baptist church life. Several Associations were formed—or in a few

[10] See W. T. Whitley, " Association Life till 1815." *Transactions of the Baptist Historical Society*, V, pp. 19-34 and E. A. Payne, *The Baptists of Berkshire*, 1951.

cases reconstituted—in the eighteenth century. Still more came into existence in the nineteenth century, and it is the twenty-seven Baptist Associations which form the basis of the Baptist Union. This is worthy of emphasis, for it is sometimes suggested that the Union simply links together individual churches,[11] while certain modern developments, like that of personal membership, have tended, probably unfortunately, to obscure what should be its real nature and function. Even now, however, half the membership of the Council which conducts the business of the Baptist Union consists of representatives appointed by the affiliated Associations.

How Associations of Churches have been regarded in Baptist circles may be judged by two or three quotations. The Circular Letter of the Eastern Association for 1777 undertakes a formal exposition of their nature and purpose, daringly setting them on a level with ordinances of the Church such as Baptism and the Lord's Supper. Baptist churches aim, it is urged, at "the revival of primitive Christianity." "What we wish at present more particularly to recommend to you is this branch of primitive discipline *Associating*, which, we think, although it hath been degraded from its pristine dignity, and corrupted into an engine of the most savage inhumanity, is yet as capable of restitution as baptism, or the Lord's Supper, or any other primitive institute" (p. 6). Reference is made to the value of the guidance of the first Christian churches by the apostles and to the importance of the Council of Jerusalem (Acts xv.). Mosheim, the eighteenth century church historian, is quoted for the view that synods and councils were common in the second century A.D.; rather, argues the letter, they were a part of church life from the very beginning, but unfortunately they became corrupted, first, by assuming a coercive power and authority which should

[11] See, e.g. Dakin, *op. cit.*, p. 19.

have been alien to them, and, secondly, by confining their membership to ministers or clergy. It is pointed out that "as soon as ever liberty of conscience was granted," that is, in 1689, Baptists came together in a general assembly, and at the time of writing, nearly a century later, they are organised in a number of convenient Associations, each of ten or fifteen churches. What is needed is a union of these provincial associations with an annual, or perhaps, triennial, assembly of delegates chosen therefrom. This, it may be noted, would result in an organisation rather more presbyterian or synodal than the present Baptist Union, which was first formed in 1813, reconstituted in 1831 and further reorganised in 1863. The 1777 Letter goes on to plead for a more general assembly of all the Nonconformist denominations. Fifty years earlier the London ministers of the Presbyterian, Congregationalist and Baptist denominations had formed an organisation, and in 1732 the Committee of the Dissenting Deputies (which included laymen) began its work in the metropolis. But these were only London organisations. The bold project of the Eastern Baptist Association had to wait for fulfilment till the formation of the National Free Church Council in 1892.

That this Circular Letter of 1777 represented the general standpoint of those responsible for the revival of the life of the Baptist Associations in the closing decades of the eighteenth century is confirmed by the fact that in 1779 it was substantially reproduced and elaborated in the Circular Letter of the Kent and Sussex Association. Almost equally significant is the fact that John Rippon in 1790 opened his *Baptist Register*—the earliest of Baptist magazines—with a lengthy poem on "The Association" by Benjamin Francis. This may not be great poetry but it is a clear indication of the large place which the Associations and their annual gatherings had in the Baptist consciousness.

" No worldly motive, and no base design
But love of truth and purity divine,
With pious zeal for the Redeemer's cause,
That first conven'd thee and ordain'd thy laws,
While Christian friendship joined her aid apace,
To give thee strength, stability and grace. . . .
So, yearly, meet, from parts remote, in Thee,
When summer smiles on every herb and tree,
Th'associate brethren, pastors, deacons, friends,
And the full crowd that in thy train attends. . . .
O blest assembly ! . . ."

One may further note how much space was given in the *Register* to the Letters and Breviates of the Associations, and those not only of this country, but of America, where also from the beginning they were an essential part of Baptist life.

Only one nineteenth century witness need be called. So doughty a Baptist as Charles Stovel, writing in 1835, declared : " One great, and most important object in these days, is to give an effective character to the different associations." And that he intended the adjective " effective " to have real content is shown by the fact that he recommended the special study of the Epistles to Timothy and Titus, " for each of these individuals were entrusted with that kind of superintendence which is now held by the whole association " (*Hints on the Regulation of Christian Churches,* p. 163).

To sum up : these various citations make clear that from the seventeenth century Baptists have regarded the visible Church as finding expression in local communities of believers who constitute themselves churches by the election of officers, the observance of Baptism and the Lord's Supper, and Christian discipline, and who find an extension and expression of their life in free association, first, with other churches of their own faith and order, but also with all other groups of Christians loyal to the central truths of the apostolic Gospel. This, in outline, is the Baptist doctrine of the Church as visible.

It is something very different from the exaggerated independence, self-sufficiency and atomism which have sometimes been favoured of recent days. It is high churchmanship in its emphasis on the faith which is presupposed by the local covenant and by the rite of baptism, which since the days of Smyth has often taken the place of the latter. It is high churchmanship in its assertion of the Lordship of Christ and the " Crown Rights of the Redeemer." It is high churchmanship in its loyalty to " the ordinances of the Gospel "—ministry, sacraments and discipline. It is high churchmanship in its inner urge towards communion, fellowship and unity with all those other Christians who together make up the Church Catholic.

Chapter Three
THE MINISTRY OF THE CHURCH
I

THE annual Baptist Assembly at Liverpool in 1930, on the motion of the Baptist Union Council, adopted a reply to the Reports of the World Conference on Faith and Order held at Lausanne in 1927. In the course of it the following sentences occur : " We cannot agree that the ministry, as commonly understood, is essential to the existence of a true Christian Church, though we believe a ministry is necessary for its highest effectiveness. We think of the function of the ministry in terms of leadership rather than of government and discipline. We believe that, while we should frankly discuss our differences, at this time it may be a gain to emphasise our agreement on the permanent and essential marks of the Church." (*Report of the Council*, 1930, *pp.* 38-39; *Convictions*, ed. by L. Hodgson, 1934, p. 62).

A reference to the Lausanne Reports will show that this comment had reference to the section in which it is declared :

> " The Church on earth possesses certain characteristics whereby it can be known of men. These have been, since the days of the Apostles, at least the following :
>
> (1) The possession and acknowledgment of the Word of God as given in Holy Scripture and interpreted by the Holy Spirit to the Church and to the individual.
>
> (2) The profession of faith in God as He is incarnate and revealed in Christ.

(3) The acceptance of Christ's commission to preach the Gospel to every creature.

(4) The observance of the Sacraments.

(5) A ministry for the pastoral office, the preaching of the Word, and the administration of the Sacraments.

(6) A fellowship in prayer, in worship, in all the means of grace, in the pursuit of holiness, and in the service of man " (*Faith and Order*, 1927, edited by H. N. Bate, p. 464. Cf. E. S. Woods, *Lausanne*, 1927, p. 68-9).

The Baptist Union Council apparently accepted the first four marks of the Church and the sixth, but expressly denied the fifth. This was perhaps the result of a traditional and healthy reaction from the view implied by the phrase " No bishop, no church ", but it was surely a very strange exception to make, and can hardly be excused by the phrase in the reply qualifying the word ministry—" as commonly understood." Report No. III from Lausanne has in it no more about the ministry than the sentence quoted above. On Report No. V, which deals explicitly with the ministry, the Council said little more than that Baptists " do not confine the administration of Sacraments to ordained ministers, nor stipulate for the laying on of hands."

One of the aims of this chapter will be to show that whatever is the view of present-day Baptists, their predecessors of the seventeenth and eighteenth centuries would have accepted wholeheartedly the Lausanne declaration regarding the ministry as essential to the church ; that they would have reserved to the ministry—" as commonly understood "—presidency at the Lord's Table ; and that in ordination services the laying-on of hands was general among them. Further, evidence will be submitted to show (1) that the presence of other ordained ministers at ordination services was one of the ways in which the larger aspects of Christian fellowship were recognised and safeguarded, and (2) that the ministry among Baptists was not, as has recently been alleged by Dr. Dakin (*op. cit.*, pp. 44f) confined to the pastoral office. Incidentally, it will be made clear that when Baptists found a place in the ranks of their ministers for those still engaged, part-time at least, in so-called secular callings, they were not intending thereby to lower the standards of entry into the ministry or to alter its status.

II

The seventeenth century Confessions and other records make it clear that no company of believers would have been regarded as properly constituted as a church or in a full church-state until officers or ministers had been chosen. The church meeting at Glasshouse Yard in London sent into Wales a letter advising against the multiplying of churches unless the brethren there were able to provide efficient pastors.[1] An Association meeting in Southampton in 1690 specifically enjoined the speedy appointment of officers in local churches and sought the presence of Benjamin Keach and other Elders from London to ordain and to regulate local affairs.

Here Baptists of both the Arminian and Calvinistic theological traditions were at one. Where they differed was as to the orders of ministry as set out in the New Testament. Smyth's last Confession asserts:

> " 75. That the preaching of the word, and the ministry of the sacraments, representeth the ministry of Christ in the spirit; who teacheth, baptiseth, and feedeth the regenerate, by the Holy Spirit inwardly and invisibly.

[1] See Thomas Richards, *The Puritan Movement in Wales*, p. 206.

"76. That Christ hath set in His outward church two sorts of ministers: viz., some who are called pastors, teachers or elders, who administer in the word and sacraments, and others who are called deacons, men and women: whose ministry is, to serve tables and wash the saints' feet" (McGlothlin, *op. cit.*, p. 80).

Three things are to be noted here: first, the character assigned to the ministry as representing Christ, secondly, the inclusion within it of deacons as well as pastors, teachers and elders, and thirdly, the admission of women to the diaconate. The liberal attitude of the early Baptists to the ministry of women is specially notable. Though this is not provided for here, there were in England in the seventeenth century not a few women preachers among the Baptists. Dr. Rufus Jones has drawn particular attention to their work (see *Studies in Mystical Religion*, p. 419). Women like Sister Hazzard, of the Broadmead Church, and Katherine Peck, of Abingdon, were staunch leaders in times of persecution.

Helwys's Confession follows much the same lines as Smyth's, with two interesting and important additions. There is, first, a clause regarding the election of church-officers which is to be " with fasting, prayer and laying-on of hands." Secondly, it is asserted that " the officers of every church or congregation are tied by office only to that particular congregation whereof they are chosen; and therefore they cannot challenge by office any authority in any other congregation whatsoever except they would have an Apostleship " (McGlothlin, *op. cit.*, p. 91). Here there seems to be the germ of the later General Baptist office of " Bishop, or Messenger," as distinct from those of Pastor and Deacon. The Confession of the thirty congregations which joined together in 1651 stresses the fact that those who are chosen ministers should be adequately supported by the free-will gifts of the churches, but that they should in turn be ready on occasion to work with their hands. " Fasting and prayer," it is said, " ought to be used, and laying on of hands, for the ordaining of servants or officers to attend about the service of God " (McGlothlin, *op. cit.*, pp. 105, 108). " The Standard Confession of 1660 " asserts that those are owned as " Ministers of the Gospel " who are deliberately chosen and ordained " to exercise their gifts not only in the Church but also (as occasion serves) to preach to the World " (*ibid*, p. 113).

It is in the so-called " Orthodox Creed " of 1678, drawn up at a time of great suffering for all Dissenters, when it was desired to emphasise points of agreement rather than difference, that there is to be found the most fully articulated General Baptist statement regarding the officers of the church. They are, it is said, of three kinds : (1) Bishops, or Messengers, (2) Elders, or Pastors, and (3) Deacons, or Overseers of the poor. " Bishops " are to be chosen " by the common suffrage of the church, and solemnly

> set apart by fasting and prayer, with imposition of hands, by the bishops of the same function, ordinarily, and those bishops so ordained have the government of those churches that had suffrage in their election, and no other ordinarily ; as also to preach the word, or gospel, to the world, or unbelievers. And the particular pastor, or elder, in like manner is to be chosen by the common suffrage of the particular congregation and ordained by the bishop or messenger God hath placed in the church he hath charge of ; and the elder, so ordained, is to watch over that particular church ; and he may not ministerially act in any other Church before he be sent, neither ought his power, or office, any way to infringe the liberty, or due power, or office of his

bishop. . . . The deacons are in like manner to be
chosen by election and ordination, and are in their
particular congregations, to receive the charity and
free benevolence of the people " (McGlothlin, *op.
cit.*, pp. 146-7).

Bishops and elders are entitled to proper maintenance.
It is they who baptise and preside at the Lord's Table.
It is in their hands that " the discipline and government
of the Church " rests. Clearly, the bishops or messengers,
of whose work some details may be found in the pages
of Dr. Whitley's *History*, exercised functions analogous
to those entrusted of recent years to the General Superintendents appointed by the Baptist Union.[2]

The Particular Baptists, instead of a three fold order
of ministry, favoured in general a two fold one, that of
Elders or Pastors (occasionally using the title Bishops)
and Deacons. Their polity, as we have already seen, was
more like that of the Independents, with stress upon the
local church, each with its own officers, yet all the members sharing in matters of discipline. Nevertheless, they
explicitly asserted the right and duty of calling out from
the local church persons " to prophesie . . . and so teach
publickly the Word of God " (1644 Confession.
McGlothlin, *op. cit.*, p. 186), and also " to send forth
such brethren as are fitly gifted and qualified through
the Spirit of Christ to preach the Gospel to the World "
(1656 Somerset Confession. McGlothlin, p. 211-12).
These preachers were not tied to any one church, but
exercised a wide and successful evangelistic ministry, as
is clear from the growth of the Baptist movement during
the middle decades of the seventeenth century. Among
the Particular Baptists appointment both to the pastoral
office and to the diaconate was marked " with imposition

[2] Cf. also *The Minutes of the General Assembly* (edited by
Whitley), I. pp. xxviiif., 67, 70, and Thomas Grantham,
Christianismus primitivus, 1678.

of hands of the Eldership of the Church, if there be
any before constituted therein" (1689 Confession.
McGlothlin, *op. cit.,* p. 266). It seems always to have
been customary for as many neighbouring pastors as
possible to gather to join in ordination services.[3] The
records in old Minute Books and later in the *Baptist
Register* and the early issues of the *Baptist Magazine*
show that both pastors and deacons were " ordained "
with " the laying on of hands " at least until the early
years of the nineteenth century.

III

The principles involved in the statements of their Confessions long determined Baptist theory and practice. The
attitude to the ministry and the manner of entry into it
in the eighteenth century are made clear from a number
of sources. Only a few illustrations can here be given.

One of the most interesting cases is that of Andrew
Fuller. He first spoke at one of the services in his native
Soham in 1771. The church was then pastorless, one
of the deacons leading the worship each Sunday. Two
years later " the work of opening the Word on Lord's

[3] Cf. Fuller, "On ordination," *Theological and Biblical
Magazine,* 1804-5; *Works,* 1832 edition, V, pp. 280-286. The
term was used of deacons as well as ministers until the mid-
nineteenth century. Cf. C. H. Spurgeon, *The Metropolitan
Tabernacle,* 1876, pp. 59, 83 (where there is an allusion to deacons
in " semi-clerical dress "). Note Horton Davies, *The Worship
of the English Puritans,* 1948, ch. xiii, " Puritan Ordinations."
For Congregational theory and practice see Isaac Watts's Letter
to the Mark Lane Church, 1702 (Milner, *Life, Times and
Correspondence,* p. 187); Doddridge, Appendix to Ordination
Sermons dated 18 Septemeber, 1745; A. W. W. Dale, *Life of
R. W. Dale,* 1899, p. 94; and also J. S. Whale, *The Ministry
and the Sacraments,* 1937, p. 214: " Ordination to the ministry is
a spiritual act of the whole Church, and though entirely within
the competence of the local Church, it invariably takes place in
the presence of and with the assistance of representatives of other
gathered Churches." Cf. Lindsay, *Church and Ministry in the
Early Centuries,* p. 330.

days was wholly committed to Bro. Fuller, though not yet publicly sent into the ministry." In January, 1774, following a request that he should preach a funeral sermon, he was " called to the ministry " (the phrase is his own) and from then onwards did his preaching from the pulpit. Another seven months passed before " the church requested Bro. Fuller to take the pastoral care of them," and he was not " ordained pastor " till May, 1775. The " ordination " (again the word is his own) was conducted by Robert Hall, of Arnesby. A number of other ministers were there. It included the laying-on of hands.

Clearly there is here implied a wider conception of the ministry than the solely pastoral, and ordination is held to involve the presence of ministers, or pastors, from other churches. Even more significant is what occurred a few years later when the church at Kettering began to desire Fuller as its pastor. The first soundings were made in 1779 and the discussions relating to the matter occupied three years. It never occurred to Fuller that this was a matter simply between himself and Kettering, or between Kettering and Soham. It concerned the Baptist churches in the neighbourhood, and the matter was repeatedly submitted to the leading ministers of the Association. At one point the whole question was referred to Robert Robinson, of Cambridge. Similar discussion took place in 1785 among the General Baptists of the New Connexion as to whether Dan Taylor should move from Halifax to London.

Similarly, in the case of William Carey. The Church Book at Olney, under date August 10, 1786 states: " This evening our Brother William Carey was called to the work of the Ministry, and sent out by the Church to preach the Gospel, wherever God in His providence might call him." Three months later, the Moulton Church book has this entry : "Agreed universally to call our Minister Mr. Carey to the office of Pastor, which was accordingly done—and Consented to on his Part." That is to say, the term "minister" was used in a wider sense than that of "pastor." This is confirmed by the striking passage on the work and character of "a Christian minister" which occurs in Carey's *Enquiry* (p. 72). "He engages," says Carey, "to go where God pleases, and to do, or endure what He sees fit to command, or call him to, in the exercise of his function."

Precisely similar is the case of Samuel Ruston, of Hamsterley, Durham, whose call to the ministry is described in the *Baptist Register*, II, p. 483. First, he was called "to exercise his talents before the church alone on the Lord's day evenings." Next, "the whole church unanimously agreed to call him to the work of the ministry," and at a special service "the church's call of him to the ministry, to preach the word and baptise those who were proper subjects, under the direction of the church, and as eligible to the pastoral office, when called to it, was announced."

How Baptists described the authority and work of the minister may be seen Nehemiah Coxe's *Sermon preached at the Ordination of an Elder and Deacons* in 1681; from Hercules Collins's *The Temple Repair'd or An Essay to revive the long-neglected Ordinances, of exercising the spiritual Gift of Prophecy for the Edification of the Churches, and of ordaining Ministers duly qualified*, issued in 1702; from Daniel Turner's *Compendium of Social Religion*, which first appeared in 1758 and of which a second enlarged edition was issued in 1778; and from the relevant sections of Dr. John Gill's *Body of Practical Divinity*. Nehemiah Coxe was, from 1676 until his death in 1689, joint-pastor of the important church meeting in Petty France. Hercules Collins was another well-known London Baptist minister of Restoration times who suffered imprisonment in Newgate gaol. Daniel Turner was minister in Abingdon from 1748 till his death in 1798. He was the friend of Isaac Watts, and later of Robert Robinson and John Rippon, and exercised a very wide influence throughout the Midland counties. The memorial tablet in the Abingdon chapel describes him as " the scholar, the poet, the Christian." John Gill was a learned commentator and expositor whose work was very highly regarded in Baptist circles and beyond. He stood for a high, even hyper, Calvinism.

" There are necessary ordinances to be administered in the Church of Christ till the end of the World, therefore Ministers are necessary," wrote Collins. " The word of Reconciliation is committed to them, the Administration of Baptism and the Lord's Supper. All these are necessary in the Church, and therefore all Churches ought to imitate the Apostles who took a special care for a standing Ministry in the Church " (*op. cit.*, p. 51). Collins was ready to speak of ordination as " a gospel-ordinance." " Ever retain," he said, " and never part with that Rite and Ceremony in Ordination of Imposition of Hands, with Prayer, on the Person ordained " (pp. 58, 59).

Half a century later, in language that sounds very modern, Turner claimed that each particular local church is a part of " the universal church." He pleads for the keeping open of the Lord's Table to all " who appear to love our Lord Jesus Christ in sincerity " (*op. cit., p.* 174) and for regular joint Communion Services between different branches of the Church; he asserts that " every regular member and minister of the word, in any particular church, is in fact a member and minister of the Church universal : and though under special obligations to that particular church, yet hath a right to commune with, or minister to any other upon all proper occasions, as parts of the same whole " (*ibid,* pp. 9-10). Turner regards the union of particular churches for the promotion of their common interests and the maintenance of

their " purity " as " oftentimes necessary, or at least
prudent," though such unions must not " assume arbitrary
jurisdiction over the local church " (*ibid*, pp. 46-7).
" That there be some," he says, " one or more in every
particular church, invested with official power, is
necessary, and of divine appointment, for the due
administration of the word and sacraments ; the main-
taining due order in the church, and due execution of
the laws of Christ " (*ibid*, pp. 49-50). " It is to be
wished," he continues, in words which have been unconsciously echoed in the recent Polity Report, "that those
churches, who allow themselves to continue long without
a settled ministry amongst them, would seriously consider,
how clearly the scriptures . . . not only point out its
utility and importance, but prove it a divine institution,
with which it must be very wrong and dangerous to
trifle. For though they may have occasional supplies,
yet they have no right to expect the like measure of the
divine presence and blessing from them, as from a settled
ministry ; nor indeed any blessing at all, if they use
the former to the sinful neglect of the latter " (*ibid*, pp.
51-2). The ordinary officers of the church are "(at least)
bishops (sometimes called pastors and elders) and
deacons " (*ibid*, p. 55). " They are to be ordained, or
solemnly set apart and appointed to their work (usually)
by the assistance of other officers of chief power and
authority in the churches " (*ibid*, p. 67). " As to the
imposition of hands in ordination, it seems to be at least
a very convenient and proper rite upon such occasions ;
and as far as I can find constantly used in the primitive
church " (*ibid.*, p. 70).

Gill deals with the Church and its officers in Volume
III of his *Body of Practical Divinity*, which appeared
in 1770, not long before his death. He begins with an
exposition of the idea of a gathered church not essentially
different from that which John Owen, the Independent,

had put out a century earlier. The primitive church, Gill
urges, had as officers (1) apostles, prophets and
evangelists but these offices are now extinct, and (2)
pastors and deacons—offices which continue. For a man
to come to the pastoral office there must be a call, both
inward and outward. He must be a member of the church
to which he is to be ordained as pastor. " To the public
instating of him into his office, it is necessary there
should be a recognition and repetition both of the
church's choice and call of him, and of his acceptance of
it, for the confirmation thereof, and for the satisfaction
of ministers and churches in communion; who meet to
see their order, and to assist, especially the former, by
prayer for them, and by giving a word of exhortation
to them, if desired " (III, p. 265). Ordination is to
office in the particular church alone, however, and Gill
favours "a stretching out of the hands" as signifying
choice or election, rather than "an imposition of hands"
that is, Χειροταονί rather than Χειροθεσία. The latter,
he thinks, was limited to the apostles and was used by
them only on certain special occasions, as, for example,
at the appointment of the first deacons.[4]

Gill answers with a negative certain questions which
agitated the churches of his time. (1) A pastor may *not*
officiate as such in another church or administer the
Lord's Supper. "A man can never act as a pastor,
where he is not so much as a member . . . and, in consequence, cannot administer the Lord's Supper in it, which
is an act of office-power" (pp. 276-277). This issue had
troubled the Bedford church in 1662. (2) A church may
not depute a private member to administer the ordinance

---

[4] The distinction made by Gill had been the subject of controversy between Puritans and Separatists in Holland. See R. P.
Stearn, *Congregationalism in the Dutch Netherlands*, 1940, p. 117
et cet. The interpretation of *Acts* vi. 1-6, xiv. 23, *Didache* xv. 1
et cet. has never been easy. Cf. R. W. Dale, *Manual of Congregational Principles*, p. 68.

of the Lord's Supper. "As Dr. Owen observes, it would render the ministry only *convenient,* and not absolutely *necessary* to the church, which is contrary to the institution of it" (p. 279).[5] (3) A pastor may *not* remove from one congregation to another if it is for worldly advantage. He may only do so "when it appears to be for the good of the interest of religion, and of the Church of Christ in general; but this should not be without the consent of the church of which he is pastor : nor without the advice of other churches and ministers" (p. 280). The principal work of the pastor, in Dr. Gill's view, is the feeding of the Church of God committed to his care. He is *not* to feed "dogs that worry the flock . . . nor swine . . . nor the world's goats" (*op. cit.,* III, 271). Here comes out the hyper-Calvinism of the eighteenth century, the attitude of mind which made old John Ryland say to Carey, "Sit down, young man! When God wants to convert the heathen, He'll do it without your help or mine." Dr. Gill expressly excludes deacons from preaching and the administering of the ordinances.[6] They are to prepare business for church-meetings. They are to "serve tables"—"the Lord's table," "the minister's table," "the poor's tables" (*op. cit.,* p. 291).

Turner and Gill are clearly not in agreement on all points, but both have a high doctrine of the ministry and regard it, as did Collins, as an essential part of the order of a true church.

Throughout the eighteenth century it continued necessary for many a man exercising ministerial functions, whether as a "messenger" or as a "paster," to obtain

[5] See, e.g. *The True Nature of a Gospel Church,* 1689, pp. 92f, 137, etc. Cf. Savoy Declaration, 1658, XXXVIII, iv. and Thomas Goodwin, *Works,* XI, p. 416.

[6] Note that in 1810 the General Baptists of the New Connexion expressly resolved that ordination to the deacon's office "certainly confers no right" to administer the Lord's Supper.

part of his support from some " secular " calling.   Dr. Whitley, writing of the preceding century, says that " the great majority of Baptist ministers earned their own living " (*History of British Baptists*, p. 152).[7] Perhaps this was still true.   Baptists were not a very numerous or wealthy people, and could not raise large sums for ministerial support.   Dissenters generally still suffered many civil and social disabilities and handicaps.   But enough has already been said to show that office in the church was most solemnly regarded.   The calling out of men to be pastors or evangelists was no light thing. When Nathaniel Overbury, the woolstapler, was made Baptist pastor in Tetbury in 1721, or when Carey, the shoemaker, was ordained at Moulton sixty years later, it was not because the office was carelessly regarded or because the churches wanted ministers on the cheap. Overbury and Carey were, of those in their midst, the most fitted spiritually for office within the church.   Had their congregations been able fully to support them they would probably have done so.   When Robert Robinson, of Cambridge, became a farmer, when Elisha Smith, of Blockley, entered the silk trade, or when Ash, of Pershore, Ryland, of Northampton, Sutcliff, of Olney, and Gray, of Chipping Norton, opened schools, it was the better to support themselves and so to fulfil their ministry, and it was done—in most of these cases—with real reluctance.   The ministerial records of these men will stand comparison with those of any of their con-temporaries, and not least those of the clergy of the Established Church.[8]

[7] Nor were they alone in this.   W. Haller, *The Rise of Puritanism*, 1938, p. 38, refers to a Puritan divine who was " a householder, a farmer, a figure in the countryside, a preacher, a pastor, a reformer, a head of a boarding school, a husband and a prolific begetter of children."

[8] Cf. the present-day attitude of the Disciples of Christ as described by Dr. William Robinson in *The Ministry and the Sacraments*, 1937, pp. 267-8.

IV

Many important developments in Baptist practice
followed upon the founding of the Baptist Missionary
Society in 1792. Its leaders were treading uncharted
paths at home as well as abroad, but they were men of
common sense and they believed in the guidance of the
Holy Spirit.

Carey was valedicted from Leicester in the spring of
1793, and it was certainly not felt that he forfeited his
ministerial status, though he demitted office as pastor of
the Baptist church there. In 1795 Grigg and Rodway
were set aside for a mission to Sierra Leone with prayers
and the laying-on of hands, in conscious imitation of
Acts xiii. 1-3. Thereafter they were spoken of as
"ministers" (see, e.g. *Periodical Accounts*, II, p. 19).
Both had been trained at Bristol College. Fountain was
sent out to India in 1796 without training and is spoken
of as being accepted "as a missionary." In 1799 Marsh-
man and Grant were solemnly designated at Bristol for
missionary work, and Ward and Brunsdon at Olney.
There was later a further valedictory service in London,
and on Monday evening, May 13th, just as the party was
about to set out, the four new missionaries, together with
Fuller and Sutcliff, went into an upper chamber "to pray
together and to commemorate our Saviour's death"
(Taylor, *Biographies*, No. XV, p. 12). This was an
historic night for Baptists. It is doubtful whether,
according to previous practice, this observance of the
Lord's Supper was allowable.[9] It is important, however,
as showing a group of men, led by the Spirit of God
under the stress of new challenges and spiritual needs,
refusing to be bound by older ecclesiastical practice.
Just as the Society quickly came to speak of its
missionaries as ministers—and here the seventeenth

[9] See e.g. Thomas Goodwin, *Works*, XI, p. 417.

century Baptist Confessions and Carey's own words already quoted pointed the way—so it came to feel that the Lord's Supper might be observed by a company which was not in the strict sense a gathered church.

As the number of recruits increased, so the custom developed of both ordaining and valedicting men for service abroad. At Oxford in 1806, for example, Chater and Robinson were ordained with the laying-on of hands by Ryland, Fuller and Sutcliff. In the nineteenth century, when the title " Reverend " came to be used by Baptist pastors in this country, it was also taken by missionaries serving overseas. Both came to be known as " Baptist ministers." Charles Stovel, in his *Hints on the Regulation of Christian Churches* (1835), explicitly includes in his description of the ministry two categories : first, pastors, and secondly, evangelists at home and abroad.

Two particularly interesting ordination services took place in London in the early years of Stovel's ministry. They show the willingness of his generation to confer ministerial status on two Germans who were to return to their own land, the one as an itinerant evangelist, the other as a pastor. In 1830 at Camberwell chapel, Charles Christian Tauchnitz, of Leipzig, was solemnly set apart as an evangelist among the Mennonite churches of the continent. Thomas Price opened the proceedings. Edward Steane gave an address. Joseph Ivimey " offered the ordination prayer, accompanied with imposition of hands." Dr. F. A. Cox gave an address on the duties of the office (*Baptist Magazine*, 1830, p. 396). An even more significant service took place in 1840, when G. W. Lehmann, of Berlin, the able associate of Oncken in the beginnings of Baptist work in Germany, came to England for ordination. On this occasion, in Salter's Hall chapel, J. H. Hinton, the Secretary of the Baptist Union, gave the ordination prayer.

The growing work of the Baptist Missionary Society

presented Baptists with a further challenge necessitating departure from previous practice. When Fuller died in 1815, he was succeeded as secretary by John Ryland and James Hinton, the one pastor and College President in Bristol, the other pastor in Oxford. Hinton soon resigned and his place was taken by John Dyer, of Reading. In a few months it was clear that a full-time secretary was necessary, and Dyer gave up his pastoral service to devote his whole time to the Society. Since 1818, the Society has always had at least one, and latterly several, fully trained " ministers " at its headquarters. It was not felt that Dyer, or Angus, or Trestrail, or Bailhache, or John Brown Myers ceased to be " Baptist ministers " while they were serving the B.M.S. They always retained the title " Reverend." Similarly with those called to give their whole time to the training of ministerial candidates. In the same way, also, when the work of the Baptist Union grew so much that it required a full-time secretary, the Baptist community, with a due sense of responsibility, believing itself to be under the guidance of the Spirit of God, came to feel that one of its number, duly trained as a " minister of the Word," should be set aside for this particular task. Of recent years, at least one other " minister " besides the Secretary has been on the headquarters staff of the Baptist Union, while from time to time others have been seconded from the pastorate for special work such as evangelistic campaigns, chaplaincies, and certain interdenominational undertakings.

Moreover, the steady movement of events has been towards the linking of each individual minister with the Baptist Union as representing the whole Baptist community. Speaking on " The Christian Ministry and the Baptist Churches " at the meetings of the Baptist Union in Bradford in 1908, Dr. Charles Brown pleaded for " a vital connection between each minister and the Baptist

Union from the first to the last; that his membership in it should be worth something, and that it should assume some measure of responsibility for him." "I would like to see some men freed from pastoral cares and responsibilities and set apart for the service of the whole body," he declared (*Baptist Times*, October 2, 1908). This has come to pass increasingly. Recognition regulations and Sustentation and Superannuation Funds are but the material expression of new spiritual relationships. To see in the Baptist Union rules, as Dr. Dakin seems to do, no more than "natural obligations related to palpable benefits" (*op. cit.*, p. 57), is to miss their real significance.

These developments imply an enlarged churchmanship, but not one in any essential matter out of accord with the principles enunciated in the earliest Confessions. When Baptists realised their obligations to the heathen world they entrusted this service to the B.M.S., which thus became the expression and channel of an essential part of their churchmanship. Later on, when the Union was formed, the local churches entrusted it with certain matters vital to "the true nature of a gospel church." For a century or more, therefore, Baptist churches have fulfilled their churchmanship not only through their local worship and service, but through the Missionary Society and the Union. This has inevitably involved new applications of the doctrine of the ministry. The pastor, the missionary, the College Principal, the secretary, the chaplain, have each a place in the ministry of the Church.[10] Due recognition of special gifts and special functions has always been an essential part of true

[10] Cf. E. T. Hiscox, the American: "The Pastorate and the Ministry are related, but not identical. A pastor is a minister, but a minister is not necessarily a pastor" (*op. cit.*, p. 94). For modern statements of the position and responsibilities of pastors in a local Baptist church see F. T. Lord, "The Office and Function of the Baptist Ministry," *Baptist Quarterly*, VIII, 1926, pp. 99f. and R. L. Child, "The Christian Pastor," *ibid*, XI. 1945, pp. 330f.

churchmanship. Those who, like the Baptists, seek to base the foundations of their polity on the New Testament, can appeal to the great Pauline passages, 1 Corinthians xii. 28-31, Romans xii. 5-8, and Ephesians iv. 11-12, with their lists of the varied gifts bestowed by the Spirit for the leadership, discipline and service of the Church. Apostles, prophets, evangelists, pastors, teachers—all are required " for the equipment of the saints, for the business of the ministry, for the up-building of the Body of Christ " (Moffatt, Eph. iv. 12).

Chapter Four
THE LORD'S TABLE
I

CHURCH officers, duly chosen and commissioned, were regarded as necessary to the proper functioning of the church. Of that there can be no doubt after a study of Baptist records. One of the chief tasks of the ministers of the church has always been reckoned to be the due observance of the Lord's Supper. In the historic *Broadmead Records* this entry occurs : " In the year 1670 the Church did not break bread until we had another pastor. The elders forbore to break bread, that holy ordinance, till they had a pastor, whose proper work it is to administer the same." In a letter addressed to the church at Whitchurch, in Hampshire, an Association meeting at Broughton in 1691 declared : " In order to your furtherance in so good a work we have been seriously debating the matters in question (to wit) what it is that regularly capacitates a person to administer the Lord's Supper. Resolved, that it is his being set apart by ordination as we humbly conceive, there being no Scripture precept for or precedent of it being administered by any other person."

The custom of a deacon or a so-called " layman " presiding at the Lord's Table in the absence of a pastor or an ordained minister, except in rare cases of emergency, appears to have been almost unknown in Baptist churches until the middle of the nineteenth century. It grew up as the number of separate fellowships increased and when, but for the help of laymen, certain groups would have been deprived of the Lord's Supper. Baptists were influenced by the practice of some of the Methodist churches and by a healthy reaction from the priestly claims of the Tractarians. But it was recognised that only the pastor presided at the Lord's Table by right of office. Others had to be specifically requested to do so by the local church. No man could assume the right.

Until quite recent times most churches hesitated to let even a ministerial student preside at the Table and, if the pastor was available, not even a visiting minister was allowed to do so. Of the situation at the Metropolitan Tabernacle in 1891, C. H. Spurgeon, then ill at Mentone, wrote: "I see no reason why Dr. Pierson should not preside at communion when Stott is not there. I think when Mr. Stott is there, he is in permanent office, and the Doctor is a friend supplying the pulpit" (*The Letters of C. H. Spurgeon*, 1923, p. 120). The desire, found in certain quarters today, to insist on the right of the local church to call to this service whom it will when it will, and the desire to insist that there are no ministerial functions which a layman may not on occasion exercise, are understandable. They have justification as a protest against the claims sometimes made for the priesthood in other traditions, and the doctrine of sacramental grace underlying such claims. They are dangerous, however, unless they are balanced and kept in check by a clear doctrine of the need, nature and function of the pastoral ministry.

The coming together of the members for the Communion service has always been regarded as one of the marks of true churchmanship. The Lord's Supper long had in the life of the local church a central position corresponding to that which the table itself occupied in the older meeting-houses. The Minute Books of the seventeenth and eighteenth centuries contain many cases which show how exercised were the church members when one of their number failed to "fill up his place at the Lord's Table." Beddome's *Scriptural Exposition of the Baptist Catechism* (1752) places great stress on proper preparation for Communion. Baptists no less than Christians of other traditions, have regarded this as a specially sacred place and occasion. Baptists were not represented officially at the Conference on Faith and Order at Lausanne in 1927. Had they been, it is likely that their spokesmen would have accepted the declaration that " the Sacrament of the Lord's Supper is the Church's most sacred act of worship in which the Lord's atoning death is commemorated and proclaimed, and that it is a sacrifice of praise and thanksgiving and an act of solemn self-oblation " (see Bell, *Documents on Christian Unity*, II, p. 15), though they might have hesitated a little at accepting the word " sacrament," for some of their number have always been shy of the term.

The earliest Baptist Confessions, in the sections dealing with the Lord's Supper, stand naturally close to the teaching of the great Reformers. Roman Catholic doctrine concerning the transubstantiation of the bread and wine is expressly repudiated. Here, as elsewhere, Reformers, Puritans and Separatists were agreed in seeking to recover the New Testament faith and practice. Only slowly, and not without differences on certain matters, was any new theory worked out. The three main types of interpretation which became common have been characterised by three almost self-explanatory German words—the " wunderhaft," the " historisch " and the " mystisch." They are associated with Luther, Zwingli and Calvin respectively. The great German Reformer, though he rejected Roman teaching, was still much under the influence of medieval thought and vigorously asserted the real physical presence of Christ in the consecrated elements; his theory is usually described as one of "consubstantiation." Zwingli, the Swiss, was most eager to return to the simplicities of the New Testament, and though it is often argued that he was not really a " Zwinglian " in the sense in which that term is now usually employed, yet he began a tradition that insisted on the primarily memorial character of the Lord's Supper and its significance as a means of uniting a congregation of believers in a common attestation of loyalty to their risen Lord. Calvin, the Frenchman, may be said to stand between Luther and Zwingli in this matter. " By his contemporary admirers his teaching was rightly regarded both as a spiritualising of Luther's and as a deepening of Zwingli's " (Hugh Watt,, *E.R.E.*, V, p. 567). Calvin defined a sacrament as " an external sign, by which the Lord seals on our consciences His promises of goodwill towards us, in order to sustain the weakness of our faith, and we in turn testify our piety towards Him both before Himself and before angels as well as men " (*Institutes,* IV, xiv, 1). At the Table by faith the believer and his Lord are united. Sacraments are for Calvin Sacraments of the Word and must be accompanied by the proclamation of the Word.

The influence of both Zwinglian and Calvinistic views has been strong on Baptist thought and practice. A few years ago Dr. Wheeler Robinson wrote : " The interpretation of the Lord's Supper most common amongst Baptists would be technically described as ' Zwinglian '— though it must be remembered that there was a recognition of mystical union with Christ in Zwingli's teaching which did not find full expression in his controversies. There is also a growing minority of Baptists whose interpretation of the Lord's Supper is Calvinistic rather than Zwinglian, and a growing consciousness that this rite has not taken the place amongst us which belongs to it, and that it should be celebrated with greater reverence " (*Life and Faith of the Baptists,* 1927, p. 118n). Ten years later Dr. A. C. Underwood affirmed that " Baptists stand for a *via media*, rejecting, on the one hand, all *ex opere operato* theories of the sacraments, and, on the other hand, all theories which reduce them to *nuda signa*" (*The Ministry and the Sacraments*, 1937, p. 225). More recently Dr. Dakin has committed himself to the generalisation that "Baptists repudiate altogether the notion that the service is one of memorial only" (*The Baptist View of the Church and Ministry*, 1944, p. 32). The evidence to be reviewed in this chapter suggests that all these statements require some modification. On this matter, as on many others, the diversity of the Baptist inheritance is plain. From the beginnings of Baptist witness in the seventeenth century, there have been many Baptists who have been staunch Calvinists in their interpretation of the Supper, but there have been many others who have favoured Zwinglian views. It is doubtful if either one or the other can claim to be the dominant tradition, and it is interesting to discover that it has frequently been among the Particular Baptists, that is, those Calvinistic in their attitude to questions of election, that Zwinglian views of the Lord's Supper have been most trenchantly advocated.

II

John Smyth had no scruples regarding the use of the term "Sacrament." It was applied by him both to Baptism and to the Lord's Supper. His last Confession, drawn up about 1610, appeared first in somewhat imperfect Dutch and two or three years later in English. The phrases used are of considerable interest. Smyth shows here, as on other matters, considerable independence of mind.

> " 72.   That in the outward supper which only baptised persons must partake, there is presented and figured before the eyes of the penitent and faithful,

that spiritual supper, which Christ maketh of His flesh and blood which is crucified and shed for the remission of sins (as the bread is broken and the wine poured forth), and which is eaten and drunken (as is the bread and wine bodily) only by those which are flesh of His flesh, and bone of His bone : in the communion of the same spirit.

" 73.   That the outward baptism and supper do not confer and convey grace and regeneration to the participants or communicants : but as the word is preached, they serve only to support and stir up the repentance and faith of the communicants till Christ come, till the day dawn, and the day-star arise in their hearts.

" 74.   That the sacraments have the same use that the word hath : that they are a visible word, and that they teach to the eye of them that understand as the word teacheth the ears of them that have ears to hear, and therefore as the word pertaineth not to infants, no more do the sacraments.

" 75.   That the preaching of the word, and ministry of the sacraments, representeth[1] the ministry of Christ in the Spirit; who teacheth, baptiseth, and feedeth the regenerate, by the Holy Spirit inwardly and invisibly " (McGlothlin, *op. cit.* pp. 79-80).

It is to be noted that only baptised persons were allowed to the Table and that the close linking of the Word and Sacraments, after the manner of Calvin, confirmed Smyth in excluding infants.

The later seventeenth century Confessions, both those of the General Baptists (e.g. the so-called " Orthodox Creed " of 1678), and those of the Particular Baptists

[1] These words are probably conscious echoes of Tertullian's use of *repraesentat* and *figura* in *Adv. Marcionem*, I, 14 and IV, 40.

(e.g. the 1677 Confession) were closely modelled on the Westminster Confession. They are indeed, in the main, revisions of that great Calvinistic Confession in the light of the special Baptist testimony regarding baptism. Following Smyth, the General Baptists continued to use the term "sacrament." Quite early the Particular Baptists replaced it by the term "ordinance," and where the Westminster Confession had "commemoration" used the word "memorial." This verbal change does not seem to have represented any substantial move towards Zwinglianism.[2]

An interesting and independent line of teaching comes from Bunyan. As we shall see in the next chapter, he refused to make differences of view regarding the subject or mode of baptism a barrier to Christian fellowship, and his approach to the Lord's Supper was very similar. In his *Confession of My Faith and a Reason of My Practice*, written at the end of his long imprisonment, he declared :

> " I desire you . . . to take notice; That touching shadowish, or figurative ordinances, I believe that Christ hath ordained but two in his Church, viz. Water baptism and the supper of the Lord : both which are of excellent use to the church in this world; they being to us representations of the death and resurrection of Christ; and are, as God shall make them, helps to our faith therein. But I count them not the fundamentals of our Christianity, nor grounds or rule to communion with saints; servants they are, and our mystical ministers, to teach and

[2] Note that the 1658 Savoy Declaration of the Independents uses the term "sacrament," but speaks of the Supper as a "memorial" of the sacrifice of Christ. Most Puritans preferred the term "ordinance," but as G. F. Nuttall remarks (*The Holy Spirit in Puritan Faith and Experience*, 1946, p. 90) the New Testament writers never apply this word to baptism and the Lord's Supper.

instruct us in the most weighty matters of the Kingdom of God; I therefore here declare my reverent
esteem of them; yet dare not remove them, as some
do, from the place and end where by God they are
set and appointed; Nor ascribe unto them more
than they were ordered to have in their first and
primitive institution. It is possible to commit
idolatry even with God's own appointments"
(*Works of Bunyan,* Offor's edition, II, p. 604).

Here Bunyan shows a characteristically sane and yet
reverent attitude to other sacraments, an attitude which
became widely influential in Baptist circles, particularly
in the southern midlands. It was not accepted without
controversy. William Kiffin, merchant, Commonwealth
Member of Parliament and Baptist preacher, strenuously
protested against Bunyan's readiness to sit at the Lord's
Table with those who took different sides in the "baptismal controversy," that is, with Paedobaptists as well
as Baptists. A century later Abraham Booth argued with
Robert Robinson and the Rylands over the same issue.
In the following generation the question of the right
" terms of communion " flared up again, with Joseph
Kinghorn, of Norwich, taking the more rigid side and
Robert Hall championing a wider Christian fellowship.
To certain aspects of this controversy we must return
in the next chapter. It has here to be noted that it has
occupied far more attention in Baptist circles than have
theological questions regarding the meaning and significance of the Lord's Supper itself.

III

During the eighteenth century Zwinglian views seem to
have become somewhat more general among Baptists.
The temper of the age with its suspicion of the mysterious

and inexplicable may perhaps have contributed to this.[3]

Daniel Turner, of Abingdon, whose views of the nature of the church and its ministry have already been referred to, emphasised the Lord's Supper as a bond of fellowship. The Table, in his opinion, should be open to all " who appear to love our Lord Jesus Christ in sincerity " as " a standing, visible, external pledge and means, of that divine union and fellowship all true Christians have with Christ and one another in one body, as morally distinguished and separated from the world " (*op. cit.*, pp. 173-4). In strikingly modern language, Turner argues that Christians of different views ought to be ready to meet one another at the Lord's Table, and that this would not only have " a particular and powerful tendency to subdue our mutual prejudices . . . but also more clearly evince the divine original of the church " (*ibid*, pp. 198-9). As we have seen, Abraham Booth did not agree with the opening of the Table in this manner. He was, in most matters, a rather high Calvinist. Nevertheless, in 1778, the year in which the second edition of Turner's *Compendium* appeared, Booth used strongly Zwinglian language of the Supper. " The design of the Great Institutor was that it should be a memorial of God's *love to us* and of Immanuel's *death for us*. . . . Yes, the love of God, in giving his dear, only Son ; and the death of Christ, as our divine substitute and propitiatory sacrifice, are the grand objects we are called to contemplate at the Lord's Table " (*Works*, II, p. 350).

In the Circular Letters of the influential Northamptonshire Association there do not seem to have been many

[3] Cf. F. J. Powicke in *Evangelical Christianity* (ed. by W. B. Selbie), 1911, pp. 106f, for the view that it was in the eighteenth century that Congregational churches " lapsed " into Zwinglianism. By the second half of the nineteenth century the majority of Congregationalists were Zwinglians " of the purest type." For Dale's teaching of a more Calvinistic sacramentalism and the controversies in which it involved him, see his *Life*, by A. W. W. Dale, ch. xiv.

discussions or exhortations regarding the Lord's Supper. This probably implies that it was not the subject of any special controversy. It certainly does not mean that it was lightly regarded. The Minute Books of the local churches prove that. Moreover, in the 1777 Circular Letter, John Ryland, senior, treats of " The Beauty of Social Religion," basing himself on Daniel Turner and John Gill, and incidentally quoting with approval Daniel Waterland ; baptism and the Lord's Supper are " the two positive institutions of the New Testament " and " appear to be of unspeakable importance to the glory of God and the very being of the true Church of Christ on earth " (pp 9-10). A quarter of a century later, John Sutcliff, of Olney, wrote a Letter on " The Ordinance of the Lord's Supper considered." Though he was one of the leaders of the revival and expansion of Particular Baptist churches in the midlands, his views are more definitely Zwinglian than any we have so far noted.

> " It is a standing memorial of Christ. When you see the table spread and are about to partake of the bread and wine, think you hear Christ saying, ' Remember me.' Remember who he is. . . . Again : Remember what he has done. . . . Once more : Remember where he is and what he is doing. . . . As the great high priest over the house of God, he represents the persons of all his people, and presents their services, perfumed with much incense. . . . Especially in this ordinance there is a representation of the death of Christ."

Much of Sutcliff's letter is taken up with insistence on the cardinal importance of regular attendance at the Table in obedience to the command of Christ.

It was left to Robert Hall, a younger contemporary of Sutcliff, the greatest preacher of his age and the champion against Kinghorn of a Table open to others besides those immersed on profession of faith, to protest against a merely memorial view of the Lord's Supper. It is "appointed to be a memorial of the greatest instance of love that was ever exhibited, as well as the principal pledge of Christian fraternity" (*Works*, III, p. 10). Nevertheless :

> "To consider the Lord's Supper as a mere commemoration . . . is to entertain a very inadequate view of it. If we credit St. Paul it is also a *federal rite* in which, in token of our reconciliation with God, we eat and drink in his presence : it is a feast upon a sacrifice, by which we become partakers at the altar, not less really, though in a manner more elevated and spiritual, than those who under the ancient economy presented their offerings in the temple. In this ordinance, the cup is a spiritual participation of the blood, the bread of the body of the crucified Saviour" (*ibid*, p. 45).

> "It is first a feast upon a sacrifice, in which we are actual partakers by faith of the body and blood of the Redeemer offered upon the Cross. Considered in this view it is a *federal rite*, in which we receive the pledge of reconciliation, while we avouch the Lord to be our God, and surround his table as a part of his family. In its secondary import, it is intended as a solemn recognition of each other as members of Christ, and consequently in the language of St. Paul, 'as one body and one bread'" (*ibid*, pp. 61-2).

This is high sacramental language, almost more Lutheran than Calvinist.

IV

Baptists were probably the first among English Protestants to have a special collection of hymns for use at the Lord's Table. In 1697 there appeared Joseph

Stennett's *Hymns in Commemoration of the Sufferings of our Blessed Saviour, Jesus Christ, composed for the celebration of his Holy Supper*. Stennett, who was born in 1663 and who died in 1713, was a Baptist minister of considerable literary gifts, widely respected for his learning and character. Many fruitless attempts were made during the reign of Anne to get him to conform to the Church of England. None of the fifty hymns would make much appeal to-day, but they are important evidence of the attitude to the sacrament at the beginning of the eighteenth century. Two of Joseph Stennett's communion hymns had a place in Rippon's *Selection*, the first edition of which appeared in 1787. Rippon included nineteen communion hymns, making use of some by Watts and Wesley, but drawing chiefly on Baptist writers —Daniel Turner, Benjamin Beddome, Anne Steele, and Joseph Stennett, as well as the latter's son and grandson, Dr. Joseph Stennett and Dr. Samuel Stennett. The *New Selection* of 1829 has only thirteen communion hymns, but four of the contributors were Baptists. Out of the twenty-eight communion hymns in *Psalms and Hymns*, which was first issued in 1862, only one was by a Baptist. In neither of the editions of the *Baptist Church Hymnal* (1900 and 1933) is there any hymn by a Baptist in the communion section. That may mean no more than that Baptists have not proved themselves effective hymn-writers and that the field of choice has been widened. It may, however, indicate that during the last century the service has ceased to have so central a place in the life of the churches.

That there was a change of sentiment in the nineteenth century, in this as in other matters, is clear. The German Baptist Confession of Faith, drawn up in 1847, was predominantly Calvinistic in theology, but American Baptists are said to be mainly, and sometimes rather aggressively, Zwinglian. In America, and in Britain, men and women, other than ministers or church officers, are to be found presiding on occasion at the Lord's Table. In many churches the service has become a brief appendix to one of the main diets of worship, attended by only a small proportion of the membership. In a volume of sermons which appeared in 1884, Alexander McLaren, the great Baptist expositor, declared, in striking contrast to Robert Hall : " All our theories about the meaning and value of this Communion Service must be found within the four corners of that word . . . a memorial rite, and as far as I know, nothing more whatsoever " (*A Year's Ministry*, First Series, p. 101). McLaren was perhaps provoked to this declaration by the appearance of R. W. Dale's *Manual of Congregational Principles* (1884). The " Calvinistic " section on the sacraments was unacceptable to the majority of Congregationalists at the time. When the Baptist Union replied to the Lambeth Appeal of 1920, the section on the Lord's Supper was brief and untheological, chiefly concerned to insist that the effectiveness of the " rite," as it was called, could not depend upon the " episcopal ordination " of " a celebrant." [4] In the years subsequent to the Lausanne Conference of 1927, a Theological Commission set up by the Faith and Order Movement collected a number of important papers dealing with the interpretation of the Christian ministry and sacraments by the different Christian traditions. Dr. Underwood did not feel it necessary to offer any independent treatment of the Lord's Supper on behalf of Baptists. He was ready to accept the thoroughgoing Calvinistic contribution submitted by Dr. J. S. Whale on behalf of the Congregationalists. How little serious attention has been given by Baptists of recent decades to the meaning and place of the sacrament in the life of the church may be judged from the fact that neither in the *Transactions of the Baptist Historical Society*,

[4] See Appendix B.

which first appeared in 1908, nor in its successor the *Baptist Quarterly,* issued regularly since 1922, does there seem ever to have been an article by a Baptist dealing either historically or theologically with the Lord's Supper.

The " Statement on the Lord's Supper " issued in 1951 by the Principals and Tutors of the Baptist Colleges at the request of the Baptist Union Council is therefore deserving of a warm welcome and close study. It deals with theological as well as practical issues and should help to a clearer understanding and a worthier administration of the ordinance.

Are not the words of Benjamin Beddome in his Catechism still true : " What are the outward Means whereby Christ communicateth to us the Benefits of Redemption ? The outward and ordinary Means whereby Christ communicateth to us the Benefits of Redemption are his Ordinances, especially the Word, Sacraments and Prayer, all which are made effectual to the Elect for Salvation " (*op. cit.,* Quest XCIII)? And is not the Lord's Supper still rightly described as one of the " effectual Means of Salvation "?

Chapter Five

BAPTISM

I

BAPTISTS are known by a nickname referring to their practice in regard to the second New Testament ordinance or sacrament, that of baptism. Like the term " Christian," as first coined in Antioch, and many another nickname, it is an honourable designation of which no one need be ashamed. It is, however, not nearly as apt as " Christian." It tends to distract attention from the great reaches of Christian faith and practice common to Baptists and all those of the Protestant and Free Church traditions, and is therefore frequently a source of misunderstanding. Moreover, baptism is observed by all the great Christian traditions (save those which reject all outward rites and symbols) and in not a few receives even greater emphasis, both in theory and practice, than it does among those styled Baptists. In origin the name is a shortened form of " Anabaptist," which at any rate in the sixteenth and seventeenth centuries had the virtue of accurately describing those to whom it was given. They were " rebaptisers." They repudiated the so-called baptism of infants, holding that it was not true baptism, and by encouraging men and women to submit to the rite as a sign of conscious personal faith in Christ, could fitly be described by their opponents as those who baptised a second time. After the Münster episode of 1533-5, however, the name Anabaptist had a sinister sound. It was a term of abuse, almost the ugliest that could be used throughout the following century. Those who drew up the earliest of the Confessions to which we have been referring were eager to avoid and repudiate the name. That of Smyth is on behalf of " certain English people living at Amsterdam." The 1651 Confession deals with "the faith and practice of thirty congregations gathered according to the primitive pattern." What we now describe as the Particular Baptist Confession of 1644 and the standard General Baptist Confession of 1660 are in the name of " churches which are commonly (though falsely) called Anabaptists." Those who drew up the 1677 Confession[1] speak of themselves as " Christians baptised upon profession of their faith." But a nickname once given sticks. Some kind of popular label is inevitable. For several generations the longer form " Anabaptist " continued to be used by their opponents.[2] The prefix gradually came to have less point, and at length all parties acquiesced in the shorter form.

These matters are important for the gaining of a true perspective. The pioneers of the modern Baptist movement were seeking to recover the purity and strength of the primitive church. Many of them had come by way of a long pilgrimage from the Anglican or even the Roman Church. They had been in company with other Reformers, Puritans and Separatists, until in their search for truth and their study of Scripture they became convinced that New Testament baptism was of believers only and that the root of many an abuse and corruption lay in departure therefrom. As has already been suggested,

[1] See Appendix A.

[2] Cf., e.g. John Wesley, *Journal*, 28 October, 1743, and 13 January, 1746, 4 August, 1766, 16 March, 1768 and 18 May, 1788. Note also the scornful use of the term in connection with those charged with complicity in the French invasion of Pembrokeshire in 1797, and in the Parliamentary debates on the East India India Company's charter in 1813. But the negro Baptists of Jamaica in the closing years of the eighteenth century had apparently no objection to the name (see *Baptist Quarterly*, VII., 1934, p. 24).

it is mere affectation to try completely to dissociate
Smyth and Helwys from those on the Continent who
had in the sixteenth century already come to reject the
sprinkling (or, as it came later to be called, the rantism)
of infants. The Englishmen were certainly in direct
touch in Holland with Mennonites, and they read Calvin
as well as the New Testament. There are few better
introductions to the beginnings of modern Baptist witness
than Calvin's apology for paedobaptism in the definitive
1559 edition of the *Institutes* (IV, xvi). In it may
clearly be seen both the excited and irrational prejudice
against those who rejected infant-baptism and the
involved and laboured explanations necessary to defend
it. Infant-baptism had been repudiated by Michael
Servetus, and the violence of Calvin's language is no doubt
in part due to unhappy memories of his controversies
with Servetus and the burning of the latter in Geneva
in 1553. Calvin writes of those who reject infant-
baptism as " furious madmen," " frenzied," "malignant
spirits." His defence of the practice turns almost
entirely on the equation of baptism and circumcision,[3]
and he can give no clear answer to the question why
if faith be admitted to be necessary in those coming to
the Lord's Table, it must not also be present in those
submitting to the other gospel sacrament. Both
Schleiermacher and Barth admit that Calvin's language
is much too violent for one really sure of his ground.[4]
Did he not himself define a sacrament as "an external
sign, by which the Lord seals on our consciences his
promises of good-will towards us, in order to sustain the

[3] Smyth's explicit repudiation of this will be found in his *The
Character of the Beast, or The False Constitution of the Church,*
1609 (*Works,* ed. by Whitley, pp. 563f). Cf. Beddome, *Scriptural
Exposition, etc.,* 1752, Quest. XCIX : " Doth not Baptism come
in the Room of Circumcision? No."

[4] Schleiermacher, *The Christian Faith,* p. 138; Karl Barth,
The Teaching of the Church Regarding Baptism, E.T. 1948, p. 49.

weakness of our faith, and we in our turn testify our piety towards Him, both before Himself, and before angels as well as men " (*Institutes*, IV. xiv, 1)?

When John Robinson valedicted those of his church setting out for distant America, he is said to have addressed them in these words : " I cannot sufficiently bewail the condition of the Reformed Churches, who are come to a Period in Religion and will go at present no further than the instruments of their Reformation. The Lutheran can't be drawn to go beyond what Luther saw; whatever part of His will our God has revealed to Calvin, they will rather die than embrace it; and the Calvinists, you see, stick fast where they were left by that great man of God, who yet saw not all things. . . . I beseech you remember, it is an article of your church-covenant, that you be ready to receive whatever truth shall be made known to you from the written Word of God" (Neal, *History of the Puritans*, Pt. II, ch. ii). It was in this spirit that Smyth, Helwys and the other early Baptist pioneers approached questions as to the nature of the church, its ministry and its sacraments, and not least the sacrament of baptism.

II

We do not find here, any more than on other matters, complete unanimity of view. Divergencies as to the nature and meaning of sacraments in general inevitably affect thought and practice in regard to baptism as well as the Lord's Supper. Smyth in his last Confession was clear that " the outward baptism of water " should be administered only to " penitent and faithful persons " and that " the outward supper " should be partaken of only by those so baptised. Just as the Supper " presented and figured " Christ's spiritual feeding of His true disciples, so in baptism there is " presented and figured the spiritual baptism of Christ, that is, the baptism of the Holy Ghost and fire, the baptism into the death and resurrection of Christ " (McGlothlin, *op. cit.*, p. 79). Helwys's Confession asserts that " every church is to receive in all their members by baptism upon the confession of their faith and sins wrought by the preaching of the Gospel, according to the primitive institution and practice, and therefore churches constituted after any other manner, or of any other persons are not according to Christ's testament " (*ibid*, p. 89). Both Smyth and Helwys clearly have Romans vi. in mind in their interpretation of the rite. The General Baptist Confession of 1651 emphasises the fact that New Testament baptism was by immersion and that those so baptised were " at the same time or day . . . of the visible Church of God " (*ibid*, p. 103). The 1660 Confession appears to insert other stages into the process of church-membership. First there must be teaching and preaching, then the baptism or immersion of those professing repentance and faith, next prayer and laying-on of hands that the Holy Spirit may be received,[5] then, and only then, is the believer a member of a properly constituted church (*ibid*, *pp* 115-116). The Orthodox Confession of 1678, keeping as close as its authors could to the Westminster Confession, describes the two sacraments of baptism and the Lord's Supper as " ordinances of positive, sovereign and holy institution, appointed by the Lord Jesus Christ, the only law-giver, to be continued in His church, to the end of the world :

[5] This matter was as early as 1651 the subject of controversy in certain Baptist circles. The church-covenant of Slapton (Northants) inserted in a book bearing the date 1681 provides for differences of opinion on the question of laying-on of hands. See W. G. Anderson, *The Baptist Churches at Weston-by-Weedon and Sulgrave*, 1930, pp 4-5. There were disputes on the matter in Portsmouth in 1782. Members were received by the laying-on of hands at Llanwenarth as late as 1819 and at Horsham General Baptist Church at least until 1839, though it was optional after 1829.

and to be administered by those only who are rightly qualified, and thereunto called, according to the command of Christ" (*ibid*, p. 144). Baptism is described as a sign of entrance into the covenant of grace and into the church, a sign of the remission of sin, and a sign of fellowship with Christ in His death and resurrection; but it must be administered only to those who really profess repentance and faith.

The Particular Baptist Confession of 1644 asserts that "the things signified" by baptism are: "first, the washing the whole soul in the blood of Christ; secondly, that interest the saints have in the death, burial and resurrection; thirdly, together with a confirmation of our faith, that as certainly as the body is buried under water, and riseth again, so certainly shall the bodies of the saints be raised by the power of Christ, in the day of the resurrection, to reign with Christ" (*ibid*, p. 185). A new note is struck by the assertion that baptism is not tied to a particular church or a particular church-officer, but may be administered by any disciple engaged in preaching. This practice, and the view underlying it, later exercised considerable influence in certain Baptist circles. The 1677 Confession[6] accepts the more common tradition which had been clearly enunciated by Calvin (*Institutes*, IV, xv. 20), that both the sacraments should be administered only by the duly appointed officers of the church.

These seventeenth century Confessions give clear expression to the convictions of the early Baptists. It soon became evident, however, that many of those who shared their views on the nature of the Gospel and church-polity generally were not ready to follow them on the matter of baptism. Inevitably the question presented

[6] See Appendix A. Cf. J. H. Bacoats at the Atlanta Congress: "Nearly all Baptists regard the proper administrator to be one who has received authority from the church to baptise" (*Report*, p. 177).

itself whether difference of opinion on this one matter
should be a ground of separation from church-fellowship
and, in particular, from the Lord's Table. In many
places, during the troubled periods both of the Commonwealth and the Restoration, those who separated themselves from the Anglican Church were few in numbers
and subject to violent persecution and abuse. To many
it seemed that this was a matter for the individual conscience and that it would be not only folly but iniquity
to divide on the issue of baptism those whose interpretation of the main articles of faith and practice was one.
Moreover, many scrupled to re-baptise, even if they
agreed that the earlier baptism had not been true to New
Testament practice.

The most famous exponent of this view was John
Bunyan. His words on " shadowish, or figurative
ordinances " have already been quoted. He returned to
the subject in 1673 in his lengthy and vigorous pamphlet,
*Differences in Judgment about Water Baptism no Bar
to Communion.* " The Church of Christ," he claimed,
" hath not warrant to keep out of their communion the
Christian that is discovered to be a visible saint of the
word, the Christian that walketh according to his light
with God " (Offor's edition, II, p. 617). Faith, not any
outward ceremony, must be held the means of entry into
the visible church. " I find not," says Bunyan, " that
baptism is a sign to any but the person that is baptised "
(*ibid.*, p. 619). He pleaded earnestly for a wide Christian
charity. His views were quite unacceptable to William
Kiffin and many other Baptist leaders, but there grew up
throughout Bedfordshire and the neighbouring counties
a very large number of churches which admitted to membership both Paedo-baptists and Baptists. During the
century following Bunyan probably the majority of the
churches in the midlands and the south of England were
of this type. The work of Vavasor Powell in Wales re-

sulted in similar churches there.[7]   Hence it is that in not
a few towns the modern Congregationalist and Baptist
churches have a common origin with the year of
foundation claimed by both denominations.

The attitude of their fellow Puritans to the two types
of Baptists is well illustrated by a comment of Richard
Baxter's :

> " There are two sorts of men called Anabaptists
> among us " : he writes in the preface to *More
> Proofs of Infants Church-membership,* " The one
> sort are sober Godly Christians, who when they are
> rebaptized to satisfy their consciences, live among us
> in Christian love and peace; and I shall be ashamed
> if I love not them as heartily, and own them not as
> peaceably, as any of them shall do either me or better
> men than I, that differ from them. The other sort
> hold it unlawful to hold communion with such as
> are not of their mind and way, and are schismati-
> cally troublesome and unquiet, in labouring to in-
> crease their Party. These are they that offend me
> and other lovers of peace."

This is hardly fair to the convictions of Kiffin and those
who thought with him. It is, however, important to
realize that since the seventeenth century there has been
difference of opinion among Baptists on the legitimate
limits of local church fellowship.

The tradition of " mixed, or free communion " churches
is so important that a few illustrations may be given. In
the Church Book of College Street, Northampton, the
following note was annexed to the Church Covenant in
November, 1700, and continued to be read at the reception
of new members at least until the close of the nineteenth
century :

[7] See Thomas Richards *The Puritan Movement in Wales,* pp.
197, 210, and *Wales Under the Penal Code,* ch. vii.

" And whereas we differ in our judgment about water-baptism, we do now solemnly declare, That we that are for infant-baptism do not hereby, nor will not impose on the others or any of our brethren or sisters that are among us who are for baptism upon profession of faith. And on the other hand, we that are for Believers Baptism do not, nor will not impose upon the consciences of any of our brethren or sisters that are amongst us, that are for Infant Baptism. Nor will we either party, or any of us impose upon any that hereafter may join in communion with us; but do all promise (freely and cordially, without casting reflections, etc. on the persons or practice of any) to leave every one to his or her liberty or judgment and practice herein; each of us walking conscientiously up to our light; engaging and endeavouring in the strength of Christ that our difference in judgment shall not cause breach of union or affection " (John Taylor, *History of College St., Northampton,* 1897, p.5).

In 1775 Benjamin Beddome of Bourton-on-the-Water drew up a covenant of this type for the fellowship at Chipping Norton. Five years later, in 1780, the church in Oxford was reconstituted, Daniel Turner, of Abingdon, whose views have been more than once quoted in these pages, taking a lead in the matter. The new Covenant then adopted contained the following :

" Whereas some of us do verily believe that the sprinkling of the infant children of believing parents in the name of the Father, the Son and the Holy Spirit, is true Christian baptism; and others of us do believe that true Christian baptism is that which is administered to adults upon the profession of their repentance, faith and experience of the grace of God, by immersion in the name of the Sacred Three; yet

notwithstanding this difference of sentiment, we promise and agree to receive one another into the same
affection and love; and for this, among other many
reasons : because we can find no warrant in the
Word of God to make such difference of sentiment
any bar to communion at the Lord's Table in particular, or to Church fellowship in general; and
because the Lord Jesus receiving and owning them
on both sides of the question, we think we ought to
do so " (E. C. Alden, *The Old Church at New
Road*, 1904, pp. 14-15).

The little church at Roade, in Northamptonshire,
reaffirmed a covenant of this type in 1781. At the time,
however, the new life which was beginning to show itself
in and through the Northampton Association of Particular
Baptist Churches led to a number of churches which had
been of " mixed communion " becoming stricter in their
practice. A new Covenant drawn up in 1790 for the
church at Stony Stratford, which had been founded in
1657, recorded the decision " to receive such, and only
such, into communion with us as . . . have been baptised
according to the primitive mode of administering that
ordinance." [8]   One of the articles of Religion of the New
Connexion of the General Baptists, formed in 1770,
stated :

" We believe that it is the indispensable duty of
all who repent and believe the gospel, to be baptised
by immersion in water, in order to be initiated into
a church state : and that no person ought to be
received into the church without submission to that
ordinance."

The growth and expansion of Nonconformity, and the

[8] The Covenant is printed in full in the *Baptist Quarterly*, III.
(1926), pp. 41-44,

establishment of causes in the new industrial areas in
the closing decades of the eighteenth century and the early
decades of the nineteenth, tended to be along separated
denominational lines.   The Bunyan tradition lost its
vigour.   Most of the Baptist churches of the North of
England and Wales, and the churches in and around
London formed under the inspiration of C. H. Spurgeon,
opened their membership only to those baptised on profession of faith.[9]   Some churches would receive at the
Lord's Table only those baptised as believers, thus continuing the tradition of what are now known as Strict
Baptist churches, which are strict both in their Calvinistic
theology and in their practice.

Bunyan's broader conceptions were, however, never
entirely forgotten.   In 1838 the Free Communion Baptist
Church Meeting in Crown Terrace, Aberdeen, reaffirmed
a constitution of a broad, inclusive type.   When, in 1869,
with the help of the London Baptist Association, the
Downs Chapel, Clapton, was erected, the constitution of
the church formed to meet within it stated :

> " Membership of the Church is open to all who
> confess faith in Christ.   We desire to have the
> Church as open as the Kingdom of God, and its gate
> neither broader nor narrower than that by which men
> enter into Life.   All who are members of Christ's
> body are welcome to our fellowship, irrespective of
> opinion on matters wherein we are all learners, and
> none master or lords.   We seek not uniformity but
> unity—the unity of faith in Christ—and trust the
> love of God to keep us in unity of spirit and bonds of
> peace. . . . The question of Baptism is left entirely

[9] Cf. W. Y. Fullerton, *C. H. Spurgeon,* 1920, p. 291 : " Mr.
Spurgeon's position was Calvinistic, accompanied by open Communion. . . . The Tabernacle . . . admitted people to the Lord's
Table who were not baptised, and refused them membership unless
baptised."

to individual judgment and conscience. The immersion of believers is the only ordinance taught or practised as baptism, but we make no difference in the manner of cordiality of our reception of Christ's disciples. The rule observed is—Let every man be fully persuaded in his own mind, and do according to his own understanding of Christ's will."

In the latter part of the nineteenth century and the early decades of the twentieth a large number of Baptist churches in all parts of the country opened first the Lord's Table, and then the membership, to others than baptised believers. Certain churches in the midlands, once of the mixed communion pattern, then more strict, reverted to their earlier and broader custom. The opening of membership in so wide a fashion as that described in the Downs constitution just quoted—and not a few Baptist as well as Congregationalist churches are similarly based —has resulted in recent days in there being a considerable number of persons in fellowship, and sometimes in office as deacons, who have not been baptised at all, either as infants or as professed believers. The possibility of such a situation would hardly have occurred to any of the Reformers or to the pioneers of the seventeenth century. Indeed, it was probably hardly forseen even in 1869, though by then what had earlier been known as " positive institutions " or " gospel ordinances " had begun to lose their authority over an increasing number of persons.

Whether such a situation is regarded as gravely disturbing or not depends largely on the view taken of the authority and purpose of baptism. If " spirit-baptism " is more important than " water-baptism," and if " water-baptism " should be administered only to those already in conscious touch with the Spirit, then those who have never submitted, or been submitted, to the rite are at least in no worse case than those who have been " baptised " as infants. But if the rite may not only symbolise but convey to the faithful the grace of God, and if a part of its meaning lies in its outward linking of men and women with the visible historic Church, then clearly much is lost by those who observe one of the gospel sacraments, but are content to ignore the other, and much is lost also by the local fellowship itself.

III

The very considerable variety of practice in regard to baptism from the beginnings of Baptist witness down to our own day is naturally reflected in differences of interpretation. Moreover, Baptist apologetic has inevitably tended to concentrate far more on questions of the subject and mode of baptism than on questions of meaning. In 1893, Silvester Horne set about writing a *Manual of Church Fellowship*, intended for use both in Congregational and Baptist churches, with the particular denominational principles set out in an appendix. Of his experiences in trying to discover Baptist teaching, he wrote thus in his diary : " I visited Dr. Clifford, but could not get from him any manual that contained a statement of their view of Baptism. I wrote to Dr. Angus, but received nothing more definite from him. My own Baptist deacons did not agree concerning it. Some thought it was an admission into the Church; some that it had nothing to do with the church, but was simply an individual act. So I am left to try and make some principles for this degenerate denomination " (*Life*, p. 78). Horne himself may have been clear as to the purpose and meaning of infant baptism, but it is fair to point out that of recent decades there have been among Congregationalists very wide variations in thought and practice. Should the baptism of infants be confined to the children of believers? Is it more than a ceremony of child-dedication by the parents and of public recognition by the Church of its responsibility in the matter of training? Is it fairly described, in the words of an acute Anglican, as "a picturesque and dramatic method of registering the name of the infant as an honorary member of the Christian society"?[10] If not, what more is there to be said? These questions have been agitating, and still agitate, Congregationalism, and no authoritative answer has been given to them.[11]

The differences of view regarding believers' baptism shown by Silvester Horne's Baptist deacons might be matched in almost every generation from the time of Smyth to our own. A number of illustrations of it have already been given. There have always been some ready to treat baptism as a rite of initiation, the divinely ordained means of entry into the visible church, whilst others have stressed its individual significance. The strict Calvinist, John Gill, may be quoted from the eighteenth century, as a particularly explicit exponent of the latter view. Baptism, he wrote, "is not a church ordinance".

"I mean it is not an ordinance administered in the church, but out of it, and in order to admission into

[10] N. P. Williams, *Ideas of the Fall and Original Sin*, 1929, p. 552: "The argument *a praxi ecclesiæ* is the only, but also a sufficient ground for affirming the legitimacy and laudability of Paedo-baptism: and . . . those who do not trust the instincts of the historic church to the extent which this argument requires should in logic either abandon the custom altogether or interpret it as picturesque and dramatic method of registering the name of the infant as an honorary member of the Christian society."

[11] Cf. D. W. Langridge, *Congregational Quarterly, October,* 1941, p. 313: "Baptism has dwindled to little more than a quaint and picturesque survival; a dedication, a welcome and an intercession on behalf of the precious little newcomer" ; and for an attempt to re-state and re-establish Calvin's teaching among Congregationalists and others see N. Micklem, "The Sacraments," in *Christian Worship: Studies in its History and Meaning*, 1936, J. S. Whale in *The Ministry and the Sacraments*, 1937, and the same writer's *Christian Doctrine*, 1941, especially ch. vii.

it, and communion with it; it is preparatory to it,
and a qualification for it; it does not make a person
a member of a church, or admit him into a visible
church; persons must first be baptised, and then
added to the church . . .; a church has nothing to
do with the baptism of any, but to be satisfied they
are baptised before they are admitted into Communion with it. Admission to baptism lies solely in
the breast of the administrator, who is the only judge
of qualifications for it, and has the sole power of
receiving to it, and of rejecting from it " (*Body of
Practical Divinity*, 1770, III, p. 311).

Gill believed in baptism as a positive ordinance intended to last until the end of the world. Its " ends and
uses " he describes as six-fold : (1) to represent the
sufferings, burial and resurrection of Christ; (2) for the
remission of sins—" not that that is the procuring or
meritorious cause of it, which only is the blood of Christ;
but they who submit unto it may, by means of it, be led,
directed and encouraged to expect it from Christ "; (3)
for the washing away of sin, and cleansing from it—" a
means of directing to Christ the Lamb of God," (4) for
a salutary or saving use and effect " by leading the faith
of the baptised to Christ as delivered for his offences, and
as risen for his justification "; (5) for the answers of a
good conscience through submission to an ordinance of
God, and (6) for an evidence of love to God by thus
obeying the command of Christ (*ibid*, pp. 339f).

Another interesting and important exposition occurs
in Andrew Fuller's 1802 Circular Letter for the
Northampton Association. It is entitled " The Practical
Uses of Christian Baptism." He closely links Christian
baptism with that of John the Baptist, and, unlike Calvin,
sharply distinguishes both from the rites of the old
covenant. For him baptism is " a solemn and practical

profession of the Christian religion." Baptism in the name of the Father, the Son and the Holy Spirit commits the individual to belief in the central Christian affirmations and beliefs. Immersion signifies the remission of sins by the death of Christ. " Sin is washed away in baptism in the same sense as Christ's flesh is eaten, and His blood drunk, in the Lord's Supper : the sign, when rightly used, leads to the thing signified." The whole ordinance suggests separation from the world, the separation both of the individual and of the Church, and entry into " a new state of being " (*Works,* 1824 edition, VIII, pp. 583f).[12]

Abraham Booth's verbose volumes, *Paedo-Baptism Examined* (1787), Vincent Tymms's *Evolution of Infant Baptism,* A. H. Newman's valuable *History of Anti-Pedobaptism* (1902) and many other works of less significance all focus their attention on the early centuries of Christian history and have very little to say about the meaning of the rite.

In 1864 Spurgeon preached a famous sermon against the doctrine of Baptismal Regeneration. Much of it was a direct attack on the evangelical clergy of the Church of England who seemed to Spurgeon to be committed by the Prayer Book to opinions which they could not consistently hold. The sermon was regarded as " rash and uncharitable " even by some Baptists. It resulted in months of heated controversy and in Spurgeon's temporary withdrawal from the World's Evangelical Alliance, but what was written about the rite itself was mainly negative. " I firmly believe and consider that baptism is the command of Christ," said Spurgeon, but

[12] For an interesting study of the subject emphasising very much the same points as Fuller, but with all the resources of modern Biblical criticism, see H. G. Marsh, *The Origin and Significance of New Testament Baptism,* 1941. Fuller would, however, have made very vigorous reply to Mr. Marsh's six pages attempting to leave room for the baptism of infants.

he was equally clear that "men are saved without any baptism".

It has been left to our own generation for Baptists to attempt a reasoned exposition and interpretation of their position. Dr. Wheeler Robinson's *Baptist Principles,* which first appeared in 1911 and has been many times reprinted since then, represents a notable and widely influential attempt, first, to trace the history of believers' baptism and then to defend it as "Scripturally sound, psychologically true, intellectually free, symbolically rich in meaning" (*op. cit.,* p. 73). Like Smyth, he is not afraid of the term "sacrament." In the New Testament, he argues, baptism implies a cleansing from sin, the gift of the Holy Spirit and an experiential union with Christ in His redeeming acts, deeper in meaning than words can express. The act and the experience cannot be separated; the one has a part in conditioning the other.[13] As a pendant to Dr. Robinson's work, we may note Dr. Underwood's consideration of New Testament baptism as "a dramatic representation of regeneration" (*Conversion : Christian and Non-Christian,* 1925, pp.109f).

The Baptist Union in its 1926 reply to the Lambeth Appeal of 1920 had not a great deal to say about baptism, save that Baptists administer it to those only who make a personal confession of repentance and faith and that the method of immersion "guards the thought of that inner

---

[13] Cf. J. V. Bartlet's definition of a sacrament as "a symbol conditioning a present deeper and decisive experience of the Divine grace, already embraced by faith" (*E.R.E.,* II, 377); and the statement by F. W. Patterson, of Nova Scotia, at the Atlanta Congress : "The term ordinance, etymologically, can never express the whole truth. Baptism and the Lord's Supper are ordinances, but they do not derive their validity, even chiefly, from the fact that they are ordained. It is true that they are not sacraments if, by sacrament, we mean that which in and of itself imparts grace; but to the man of faith they are true sacraments —confessions of faith, pledges of loyalty, oaths of allegiance; and to all such they are vehicles of God's grace" (*Report,* pp. 173-4).

baptism of the Holy Spirit which is central in Christian experience." [14]   In 1922, however, certain Baptist leaders conferring with Anglicans at Lambeth Palace, had accepted the view that baptism is " by the ordinance of Christ and of His apostles the outward and visible sign of admission into membership of the Church " (Bell, *Documents*, I, p. 147). The important Committee appointed by the Baptist Union Council in 1932 on the question of possible union between Baptists, Congregationalists and Presbyterians showed, when it reported five years later, that most modern Baptists would agree in regarding baptism as in some sense " a means of grace " having the authority of Christ Himself. The Committee was prepared to urge Baptists to reconsider sympathetically a more sacramental, i.e. Calvinistic, view of both baptism and the Lord's Supper. But they found themselves deeply divided as to the relationship of baptism to church membership.

There have been and there remain at least three sections among Baptists : (1) those who believe in open membership and open communion after the Bunyan pattern ; (2) those who would keep both membership and the Table for only those baptised as believers, and (3) those who feel that the Table should be open but that membership should be closed. The Report of a Baptist World Alliance Commission, presented at the Atlanta Congress in 1939, shows the same divisions to be present in the main areas where there is organised Baptist witness and accepts them as at present inevitable (*Report of the Atlanta Congress*, pp. 115f). These differences as we have shown, are to be found throughout the four hundred years of modern Baptist history. They cannot easily be resolved. They have their origin in the New Testament itself. The case for the subject of baptism being a

[14] See Appendix B.

believer is overwhelming, and this is now very generally
admitted by scholars. The exact relationship of the rite
to the experience of the Spirit and to membership of the
Church is not so clear. " Our sources," says Dr. George
Johnston, in a recent study and with reference particularly
to Acts ii. 14ff, viii. 15f, ix. 17 and x. 44, " are not con-
sistent about Baptism and the moment when the Spirit
was received." Another candid modern student has thus
expressed it : " A study of the New Testament teaching
on baptism leaves us in no doubt that it is impossible to
deduce therefrom a uniform doctrine. . . . Baptism was
in its earliest form an experience symbolised by the performance of a rite and not a rite which conveyed a fixed
interpretation." [15]

[15] Johnston, *The Doctrine of the Church in the New Testament,*
1943, p. 64. H. G. Marsh, *op. cit.,* pp. 202f. The conclusion of
Marsh's careful study is that John the Baptist, who stood in the
prophetic succession, was responsible for " an inspired interpretation of the tebilah, in which the emphasis was shifted from a
narrow racial conception to the proclamation of a spiritual Israel
prepared for the coming Kingdom wherein spiritual and moral, and
not physical, considerations alone counted "; Jesus gladly submitted
to the rite as thus interpreted, and it continued to be practised
generally, though not universally, by His followers till the time
when it was ready to provide them with a not inadequate symbol
for the baptism of the Spirit; throughout faith is regarded
as essential. On the tebilah see H. H. Rowley, " Jewish Proselyte
Baptism," *Hebrew Union College Annual,* XV, 1940, and " The
Origin and Meaning of Baptism," *Baptist Quarterly,* XI, (1945),
pp. 309f. A summary of recent discussions on the rite of baptism
by theologians of the Reformed Churches, and the Church of
England will be found, together with a questionnaire addressed to
Baptists, in *The Doctrine of Baptism,* Baptist World Alliance,
1951.

Chapter Six

WORSHIP

I

W E have considered the Baptist doctrine of the Church, the ministry and the sacraments. To gain any complete picture of Baptist thought and practice, and the pattern of Baptist piety and witness, a number of other matters require mention. What of the forms of corporate worship, apart from the Lord's Supper and baptism? What of church discipline and government? What of other aids to the development of personal character and devotion? These matters have not received the study they deserve, though for the maintenance of the life of churches they are no less important than theological trends and controversies, and the ecclesiastical issues which divide the main Christian traditions. The deepest springs of the spiritual life are to be found in the worship and fellowship of the local congregation, and it is because of recent years so many have become casual and thoughtless about these things that there is such widespread impoverishment and uncertainty in our corporate witness, with the result that our manifold activities often make so slight an impact on individuals and communities.

Satisfactory studies of the Baptist tradition of public and private worship and the means by which Baptists nurture Christian character are not easy to find. We have, perhaps, little that is distinctive to offer. Here, as elsewhere, we are in debt to the Reformers, to the Puritans, and to our fellow Free Churchmen. Baptists draw to a greater extent than they realise, even if not as fully as they might, on the riches of other traditions.

90

Nevertheless, they have a pattern and ethos of their own.
A knowledge of the way in which Baptists in the past
maintained their spiritual life may help them to discover
what is essential in our own day.

In his *Types of English Piety,* a choice and rewarding
book published some forty years ago, Mr. R. H. Coats
offered a discriminating study of three main types—the
sacerdotal, the evangelical and the mystical.   Baptists
belong emphatically to the second of these, and it is not
without significance that Mr. Coats takes Bunyan as its
chief exemplar.   Nevertheless, his main purpose is to
describe a type of personal devotion and one that is
" content to do without imposing adjuncts " to religion.
He has little to say about the life of the church in
Bedford which Bunyan joined and of which later he became pastor, or of the kind of services he conducted in
the closing decade of his life when he had a considerable
measure of freedom and popularity.   Dr. W. B. Maxwell
in *An Outline of Christian Worship* (1936) has provided a very valuable study of the liturgical forms to be
found in the various Christian traditions, east and west,
Roman and Reformed, but he has nothing to say about
Baptists.   Several of the essays in *Christian Worship*
(edited by N. Micklem, 1936) throw light on general
Nonconformist practice, but only in quite general terms.
Dr. Horton Davies's *The Worship of the English
Puritans* (1948), which offers a study of " the Puritan
and Reformed tradition of divine worship in England,
from the days of Cranmer to Watts," breaks new ground
by providing much detailed material on the worship of
the Separatists and Independents, with whom Baptists
were closely allied.   Many of his illustrations come from
Baptist sources.   He suggests that the early Baptists made
three special contributions to the worship of the English
Separatists, viz. believers' baptism, a more radical
opposition to forms in worship than most other groups,

and the method of running exposition or interpolated comment during the public reading of Scripture (*op. cit.,* p. 95). These three contributions were characteristic of the General Baptists from the time of John Smyth. In the closing decades of the seventeenth century, the Particular Baptists were responsible for another most important contribution to Nonconformist worship, viz. congregational hymn-singing.

II

An account of the manner of worship in Smyth's church at Amsterdam occurs in a letter sent in 1609 by Hugh and Anne Bromehead to a kinsman in England. It is of such interest that it deserves quotation in full :

" The order of the worship and government of our church is :

I. We begin with a prayer, after read some one or two chapters of the Bible; give the sense thereof and confer upon the same; that done, we lay aside our books and after a solemn prayer made by the first speaker he propoundeth some text out of the scripture and prophesieth out of the same by the space of one hour or three quarters of an hour. After him standeth up a second speaker and prophesieth out of the said text the like time and space, sometimes more, sometimes less. After him, the third, the fourth, the fifth &c., as the time will give leave. Then the first speaker concludeth with prayer as he began with prayer, with an exhortation to contribution to the poor, which collection being made is also concluded with prayer. This morning exercise begins at eight of the clock and continueth unto twelve of the clock. The like course of exercise is observed in the afternoon from two of the clock

unto five or six of the clock. Last of all the execution of the government of the Church is handled." [1]

This letter indicates the way in which the Bible had
become the centre and inspiration of Christian worship
in radical groups and also their emphasis on the present
inspiration of the Spirit. "All books, even the originals
themselves, must be laid aside in the time of spiritual
worship," said Helwys, contrasting what went on when
Smyth's company met with the meetings of the Ancient
Church of which Francis Johnson was pastor. The first
Baptists sought to recover the prophetic tradition of the
early Church. Their outlook was akin to that of many
of the Anabaptists and "Spiritual Reformers" belonging
to the left wing of the Continental Reformation. It is
therefore somewhat surprising to find that they rejected
the corporate singing of psalms and hymns. The Anabaptists left behind them a remarkable body of hymns,
one of the earliest collections dating from as early as
1564. This forms the nucleus of the *Ausbund*, a book
still in use among the Old Order Amish Mennonites of
the United States. Smyth and Helwys appear to have
rejected the use of the Psalter in worship. They regarded singing as a gift, only to be exercised individually.
Congregational singing did not become customary among
Baptists until the days of Keach.

Benjamin Keach was first a General Baptist, but later
became a Calvinist. He was a leader in the times of
persecution under the Clarendon Code. The Particular
Baptists were much closer to the Reformed tradition of
worship. Many of them had come to use psalms and
scripture paraphrases after the manner of the Presbyterians. Only with difficulty, however, were they led to
accept compositions that were not direct transcriptions
of biblical passages. For many years there was acute
controversy in Baptist churches over congregational

[1] See W. H. Burgess, *John Smyth the Se-Baptist*, pp. 170-171.

singing.[2] It was first allowed at the Lord's Supper, in accordance with Mark xiv. 26. Then came the use of hymns composed for days of special thanksgiving and prayer. Finally the custom was extended to ordinary Sunday worship. Keach was himself a prolific versifier, though most of his work seems to us mere doggerel. Stennett, whose communion hymns have already been referred to, was a man of better education, but none of his work has a place in modern hymnbooks. Both Keach and Stennett antedated Isaac Watts, however.

Baptist worship in the eighteenth century was similar to that of the other Nonconformist bodies. Two or three paraphrases or hymns were sung, the latter being often original compositions of the pastor, given out line by line with the right note for the tune sounded on a pitch-pipe. The Scriptures were read. Lengthy extemporary prayers were offered,[3] often by deacons or elders as well as by the minister. The sermons of the pastor were long and dealt with doctrinal themes. The Lord's Supper was observed once a month, usually as a special service in the afternoon. Those who gathered for worship often came long distances, and brought provisions with them. During the luncheon interval the pastor catechised the children, while the members of the church read books by Puritan preachers, Bible Commentaries by men like Matthew Henry and John Gill, or the works of Bunyan. Such books were usually kept in the drawer of the Table Pew. There were no services in the evening. The business of the church was often transacted at the close of one of the diets of worship or before sitting down at the Lord's Table.

As a result of the Evangelical Revival an appeal to

[2] See J. J. Goadby, *Bye-Paths of Baptist History*, 1871, ch. xii.
[3] As late as 1841 William Brock, of Norwich, could claim " concerning our public worship, that on Lord's days two hours are spent in prayer and supplication—sometimes more, and never less."

the unconverted became general in preaching. But even after the wide adoption of " Fullerism " among Particular Baptists and the growth of the New Connexion of the General Baptists, there remained, on the one hand, pockets of hyper-Calvinists, and, on the other, groups that were Socinian or Unitarian in sympathy. Both distrusted " Methodism " and " enthusiasm ". But the main stream of Baptist life was permanently and beneficially influenced by the Revival. Evening services were held in places where churches had not yet been established. Sunday Schools were organised. In 1787 John Rippon put out a hymnbook which quickly became popular in Baptist circles. It was intended as an appendix to Isaac Watts's *Psalms and Hymns,* but as it included many of Watts's compositions, together with hymns by Doddridge, Toplady and Cennick, it became in fact a substitute for Watts, and also the means whereby hymns by Baptist writers like Stennett, Turner, Robinson, Fawcett and Ann Steele were made widely known. Stringed instruments came into use to help the singing. By the time Victoria ascended the throne, the second service of the Sunday was increasingly held in the evening. The result in the case of one church—St. Mary's, Norwich, where this change took place about 1838—has been thus described :

> " An audience of a more miscellaneous kind was obtained, and the ministry inevitably assumed a more varied character. Subjects arising out of common life, or relating to public questions and prevalent social discussions, were handled in a manner calculated to interest the most careless persons, and to win their confidence in religious teachers." [4]

There were similar developments elsewhere. In the conduct of the morning service the minister was frequently aided by one or other of the deacons or elders. The

[4] *Life of William Brock, D.D.,* by C. M. Birrell, 1878, p. 116.

multiplication of churches meant that fewer people travelled long distances to their church, save in country districts.

III

The general pattern of church services has remained the same from the 17th century to the present day : scripture, prayer and sermon, interspersed with hymns. It did not change in essentials when organs replaced stringed instruments and choirs of singers appeared. The only notable recent developments have been (1) the shortening of the sermon and the prayers; (2) the occasional use of collects and set forms of prayer; and (3) the introduction—some would say the intrusion—of a special address to the children. In 1858 the hymnbook known as *Psalms and Hymns* first appeared and fairly quickly ousted Rippon's *Selection* and various other lesser known books. Forty-two years later it was itself replaced by the first edition of the *Baptist Church Hymnal*. This book was in circulation only thirty years before a revised edition was called for. In spite of their pioneering work in this field, there have proved to be few outstanding Baptist hymnwriters, and the tendency of Baptists—a wise one—has been to draw increasingly on the wider riches of Christian hymnody.

Side by side, however, with the official collections, used for Sunday worship in most Baptist churches, other books have often been secured and have come to have considerable influence on the religious outlook of many of the members. The most notable of these has been *Sacred Songs and Solos*, a compilation from various sources, mainly American, made by I. D. Sankey for the mission and revival services conducted by D. L. Moody. From a small booklet of twenty-four pages which first appeared in 1873, this had grown by 1903 to a collection of 1200 hymns, the words and tunes being many of them of a more popular and emotional type than had previously been known in Baptist services. Influences in a similar direction were exercised by the *Christian Endeavour Hymnal* (first edition 1896) and the *Sunday School Hymnary* (first edition 1905). Rippon did not draw much on the hymns of the Wesleys. When he compiled his *Selection,* the Baptist churches for which he sought to provide, were still suspicious of the Arminianism of the main stream of Methodism. Even *Psalms and Hymns,* which contained a thousand hymns in all, has only sixty-nine by Charles Wesley compared with two hundred and fourteen by Isaac Watts. Till the time of Moody and Sankey there was in Baptist circles relatively little emphasis on the moment of conversion. The modification of the older Baptist piety by the evangelicalism of the later decades of the nineteenth century was considerable. The change that took place was connected also with the work of C. H. Spurgeon, though *Our Own Hymnbook,* which the great preacher compiled for the Metropolitan Tabernacle in 1866 and which was adopted by a number of other churches, came too early to be influenced by the revivalism of Moody and Sankey. The work of F. B. Meyer among a younger generation in the closing decades of the nineteenth century and the first decade of the twentieth had also a considerable effect.

In addition to its use in mission halls and for revival services, *Sacred Songs and Solos* was adopted as the hymnbook for evening worship in a number of Baptist churches. The evening service was usually of a more popular character and aimed at reaching those as yet uncommitted to the Christian way of life and to the fellowship of the church. Special services of an apologetic and evangelistic character had become frequent in the Victorian age. Many preachers gave special series of sermons to young men, often away from church premises and in institutes and public halls. There was also a growing tendency to deal in sermons with public questions of the day. In the early years of the twentieth century "the social gospel" became a popular theme. "Brotherhoods" and "Sisterhoods" gathered together on a Sunday afternoon, in a free and easy fellowship aided by musical items often of a secular character, men and women whose attachment to the church was only loose, but who a generation earlier would almost certainly have been found in the gallery at an evening service.

The first World War brought this phase to an end. The majority of the men who came back from active service returned neither to the gallery, nor to the "Brotherhood." Going to church ceased to be for the middle and upper classes the popular convention it had become towards the close of the Victorian epoch and in Edwardian days. Baptists have been no more and no less successful than others in adapting themselves to changed social conditions and a new climate of opinion. There is now a closer correspondence between the committed membership of the churches and those attending the services than at any time since the eighteenth century. And of recent years there has been a noticeable tendency in preaching to return to themes of a more theological character and to seek a greater dignity and orderliness in worship.

The old calendar of the Christian church was built up around the great festivals of Christmas, Easter and Whitsuntide. Of these special festivals Baptists—in common with others of Puritan stock—long remained shy, not because they did not rest their faith in the mighty acts of God which the festivals celebrate, but because they wished to keep these acts in mind at every season of the year. Recently there has come a greater realisation of the value of the Christian calendar in developing a sense of continuity and fellowship and in keeping the central truths of the gospel clearly before the mind of a generation which has to begin at the beginning in learning about the faith.

Harvest has been added to the older list of festivals. It is not much more than a century since the present form of celebration was adopted, and Free Churchmen were more hesitant about it than Anglicans, Baptists more hesitant than most other Free Churchmen. The Church has now a special anniversary day; so does the minister, in many places . The Sunday school has special annual services and collections. Missionary societies and denominational and other bodies seek their own annual occasions for propaganda and appeal. Of recent years "Women's Sundays" and "Men's Sundays" have made their appearance in certain places. Some of these developments are of doubtful value and efficacy. They may distract attention from the true nature and purpose of Christian worship. They may repel instead of attract, and where they attract, they seem rarely to do so for very long. But with all these special services the general pattern of worship remains essentially the same, and it is to be noted that the order of service in a Baptist church is hardly distinguishable from that of the Congregationalists. Presbyterian churches use a metrical version of the psalms and Methodists keep in the main to the hymns of Charles Wesley, with the occasional use of forms from the Book of Common Prayer. Otherwise their services also are of the same general structure, though the Presbyterian *Directory of Public Worship* and *The Book of Public Prayers and Services for the use of the People called Methodists* are kept to more frequently and closely than the less official manuals and service books compiled by Baptists and Congregationalists.

What is provided in the usual morning service in a Baptist church may be compared with the account of the simple Sunday services for worship and fellowship described by Justin Martyr in the second century. This was the type of service favoured by the Swiss Brethren, the Mennonites and those of the Smyth tradition. Those who were or are under the influence of Calvin and Geneva, see the structure of the service in terms of a " Liturgy of the Word " not fully complete without the " Liturgy of the Upper Room," first the Word spoken, then the Word in acted symbol. Not many Baptists, even if their theology of redemption is Calvinistic, have a reasoned theory or theology of worship. They cherish freedom for the inspiration of the Spirit. At the same time many of the early Baptists, like the Christians described by Justin, regarded the " breaking of bread " as the climax of the service, and probably few modern Baptists, if challenged, would deny that " preaching that falls short of leading men to the Sacrament has missed its consummation."

Chapter Seven
SPIRITUAL DISCIPLINE

I

"LAST of all the execution of the government of the church is handled," So wrote Hugh Bromehead in 1609. Here is the germ of the Church Meeting which, some have suggested, is the characteristic contribution of Baptists and Congregationalists to the Church Universal. The local church directs its own affairs, seeking the guidance of Christ. It is competent to choose its own pastor and officers, and to discipline its members. No outside body has authority over it except with its own consent. All the members share equally in the decisions that are taken. One of the Articles of Agreement adopted by the Church at Amersham in 1675 puts these things in the following terms :—

> "To act in all differences that may or shall fall out in the Church as a Church jointly together with those officers God shall bless us with, the Lord giving the defined sentence by His word : and if Elder or Deacon or Elders or Deacons shall assume any power or prerogative above the Church and contrary to the words that the Church shall judge and the Lord by His Word shall give the defined sentence; and if any difference fall out between Elder and Member or Deacon and Member and it be brought orderly to the Church they both shall stand by and the Church shall judge according to God's Word." (*Minutes of the Ford and Amersham Churches,* p. 203.)

The oldest Church Books kept by Baptists date from Commonwealth times, though unfortunately complete records are very rare. As already noted, business was usually transacted either before or after one of the Sunday services though sometimes, even in the 17th century, a meeting was called during the week. The Church Book contained the Church Covenant and a list of the members with the dates of baptism or transfer. What was decided was entered in the Book and signed, often not only by the pastor, but by a number, perhaps all, of the members present. The business done in the seventeenth and eighteenth centuries concerned : (1) the appointment of church officers, including the pastor ; (2) admissions to membership ; (3) the support of those in need and distress ; (4) cases of discipline ; (5) the calling out of men to exercise their preaching gifts ; (6) the building and upkeep of the meeting-house ; and (7) matters, theological as well as practical, involving relationships with other Baptist churches or a local Association. Occasionally there were arrangements to be made for special days of Thanksgiving or of Fasting and Humiliation. Certain of these were observed at the call of the King. Others were decided on by local Baptist Associations or by the General Assembly.

A number of old Church Books have been reprinted in full and are invaluable for getting a picture of Baptist life in past generations. The Church Book of Bunyan Meeting, Bedford, from 1650 to 1821 was reproduced in facsimile in 1928. The records of the churches at Fenstanton (1651-94) and Warboys (1644-88), in Huntingdonshire, and of Hexham (1651-82), in Northumberland, were published by the Hanserd Knollys Society in 1844. The Church Books and Accounts of Cuddington or Ford (1688-1797) and of Amersham (1675-1800), in Buckinghamshire, were issued by the Baptist Historical Society in 1912. In none of these cases are the records complete, but the entries are most frequent for the earlier years. A number of other Church Books begun in the seventeenth century are in existence. It is very desirable that a list of them should be made and that they should be placed in proper custody, preferably in libraries. In many cases their intrinsic value as religious and social documents, as well as their age and present condition, makes it desirable that they should be transcribed or microfilmed.

Much space in the oldest Church Books is taken up with records of discipline. One of the basic ideas underlying the " gathered church " was mutual committal to one another linked with mutual care of one another. Spiritual as well as material care was to be exercised. The purity of the church which was aimed at concerned both belief and conduct. The earliest Baptist churches took doctrine seriously. It is a mistake to suggest that they eschewed credal statements or objected to subscription to creeds and confessions. Such an attitude was not widespread until the nineteenth century and has never been universal. The churches of the seventeenth century were either Calvinistic or Arminian in their main theological beliefs, and a brother or sister who, on this main issue, professed views different from those of the majority of the members was refused communion. Some churches took Hebrews vi. 1-2 as their basis and adhered rigidly to their own interpretation of the " six points " found therein. As we have seen, the practice of the laying-on of hands in ordination both to the pastorate and diaconate was general. The question whether hands should be laid on all believers after baptism was a much debated issue, and one on which local churches separated from one another. The church at Amersham, for example, believed that the rite should follow baptism and the Church Book in recording the names of those baptised notes that they " came under hands ". In the fifty years between 1780 and 1830 a considerable number of new churches came into existence because Fuller's evangelical Calvinism was

not universally acceptable and certain groups desired a
more rigid and restricted theology. Many of these
groups still exist as Strict Baptist Churches. The main
stream of Baptist life was, however, to be found in those
fellowships which had learned the dangers of heresy-
hunting and had come to believe in a more liberal and
tolerant attitude, fellowships which had recognised that
a profession of orthodoxy in belief is no guarantee of the
fruits of the Spirit. Most Baptist churches shared in this
matter in tendencies to which all the main Christian
communions were subject.

There was similarly a realisation that the disciplining
of conduct, however admirable in intention, had within
it grave dangers. In the seventeenth and eighteenth
centuries members of Baptist churches were subject to
rebuke and the church might " withdraw its communion
from them," if they absented themselves from the Lord's
Table, " failing to make good their place "; if they were
guilty of " Sabbath-breaking " or " prophaning the Lord's
Day "; if they married outside the fold; if they drank
to excess, kept bad company, danced or played cards.
Those who were charged with these things were sum-
moned to the Church Meeting to explain their conduct.
An opportunity was given for explanation and repentance. By the middle of the eighteenth century it seems to
have been generally recognised that it was neither possible
nor right to restrict marriage to those already in the
membership of Baptist churches. From early days, in
General Baptist churches, a member who had been disciplined for an offence had a right of appeal from the
local church to the Association and from the Association
to the General Assembly. In this, as in other matters,
the General Baptist polity was similar to that of the
Presbyterians and the Quakers, all these communities
having been influenced to a greater or lesser extent by the
Anabaptists of the sixteenth century.

The older inquisitorial methods of discipline broke down and gradually disappeared in the nineteenth century. The Church Meeting ceased to be a church court in any real sense and became a business meeting. In the Victorian age much time was spent on matters of property, equipment and organisation. Public questions connected with civil disabilities and moral issues in political and international affairs began to claim attention. When, in more recent days, full religious equality had been secured and the attitude of Baptists and Nonconformists on political matters became less uniform and homogeneous, the latter were no longer discussed and the Church Meeting suffered decay in many places. The care of the property and other business matters passed more and more into the hands of the deacons and church officers. A full meeting of the members became a rare event except for the annual meeting to receive reports and accounts, or on occasions when matters relating to the pastorate had to be considered. Changed social conditions and habits have made it more difficult to secure a large attendance of members at a mid-week meeting. The two World Wars accentuated these developments. So also did the growth of a more centralised denominational organisation.

Since the 1939-45 war two new tendencies have been observable. First, there has been in certain churches a return to the earlier practice of transacting on Sundays church business relating to the pastorate and the admission and transfer of members—after an evening service, or sometimes immediately before the observance of the Lord's Supper. Secondly, in a number of places efforts have been made to revive the mid-week Church Meeting by introducing general themes of Christian witness for discussion. There is wide recognition that much has been lost by the decline in the Church Meeting and that the sense of responsibility formerly attaching to church membership has been dangerously weakened. Many believe that a new effort must be made to articulate once more a definite code of Christian conduct adapted to the conditions of the twentieth century. Many feel also that a clearer conception of Christian belief should be conveyed to and adhered to by church members. The process of defining Christian ethics and Christian doctrines in terms of the modern situation may well result in a renewal of the life of the Church Meeting. It is too early, however, to say that this is actually taking place.

II

Puritan piety has never been sustained by Sunday services alone. "To sit under the Gospel once a week is not enough," as Dr. Dakin has put it. Less formal weekday meetings for Bible reading and prayer have since the seventeenth century characterised the tradition in which Baptists stand, and a midweek preaching service has often been a widely recognised and supported feature of their church life. Richard Baxter records in his autobiography that during his ministry in Kidderminster, in addition to his work on Sundays, he preached

"once every Thursday, besides occasional sermons. Every Thursday evening my neighbours that were most desirous and had opportunity met at my house, and there one of them repeated the sermon, and afterwards they proposed what doubts any of them had about the sermon, or any other case of conscience, and I resolved their doubts; and last of all I caused sometimes one and sometimes another of them to pray (to exercise them); and sometimes I prayed with them myself, which (besides singing a psalm) was all they did. And once a week also some of the younger sort, who were not fit to pray in so great an assembly, met among a few more privately, where they spent three hours in prayer together; every

Saturday night they met at some of their houses to repeat the sermon of the last Lord's-day, and to pray and prepare themselves for the following day " (Everyman edition, p. 77).

This was the general pattern of activity aimed at not only by the best of the seventeenth century Presbyterian ministers, but by Congregationalists like Watts and Doddridge in the eighteenth century, and also by Baptists —though many of the latter were more busily engaged in earning their living. There is no doubt that the prayer-meeting had a greater popularity among Independents and Baptists than among Presbyterians.

Meetings for conference and prayer were frequent among the soldiers of Cromwell's army, and in Commonwealth times they became a feature of local church life.

" Because we met in houses, divers times in the week-days," wrote Edward Terrill in the *Broadmead Records* under the year 1657, " for the Church Meetings, for to exercise the gifts of the church by way of conference, or for prayer in preparation to the Lord's Supper, once a month, or for prayer on other special or emergent occasions : these things they [i.e. the religious and civil authorities of Bristol] did not then understand or less practise, therefore they spake evil of us as seducers " (Bunyan Library edition, p. 48).

Such meetings were maintained even in the dark days when the Clarendon Code was in force. Throughout the eighteenth century whole days were occasionally set aside for prayer, special gatherings of this kind being always held when pastors and church officers had to be chosen. The General Assembly of the General Baptists, concerned at " the great decay of religion and the general want there is of a ministerial help in many churches," urged in 1724, not only that there should be special days of fasting and prayer, but that " private meetings " of members should be set up " that those amongst them who are most likely may have thereby the better opportunity to discover and improve their several capacities " (*Minutes*, I, p. 142). In Yorkshire—probably under Methodist influences—" experience meetings " were at one time popular, and from the closing decades of the eighteenth century cottage prayer-meetings became general in country districts.

In 1784 the Northampton Association issued its historic call for regular meetings, on the first Monday of every month, for concerted prayer for the general revival and spread of religion. The story of this Call has been told elsewhere.[1] It played a decisive part in the deepening of the spiritual life of the group of young ministers— Fuller, Ryland and Sutcliff among them—who responded to Carey's appeal in 1792 and formed the Baptist Missionary Society. The prayer movement in the midlands and elsewhere brought new life to many of the churches. The special monthly prayer-meeting gradually assumed a missionary character and continues to have this special intention in many Baptist churches, with prayer-meetings of a more general character in the other weeks. Never has the whole membership been able or willing to join in such meetings. They have waxed and waned in strength from generation to generation. During the last sixty or seventy years the multiplication of mid-week meetings and organizations of one kind and another, combined with a greater reserve and inarticulateness in religion, has weakened the place of the prayer-meeting in the life of many churches. The verdict of history is clear, however. Such meetings have been a characteristic expression of Baptist piety and they have created as well as registered spiritual conviction and

[1] See E. A. Payne, *The Prayer Call of* 1784, 1941. Reprinted in *B.M.S. Ter-Jubilee Celebrations*, 1942-44, 1945, pp. 19f.

power. Many of those who were the pillars of the local churches during the difficult decades after 1914 owed much of their strength of character and their gifts of leadership to the prayer-meetings connected with Christian Endeavour Societies and Young People's Fellowships in which they were trained. These had in their own way continued the tradition going back to Baxter.

III

The language of free prayer used in the prayer-meeting has always been the language of Scripture. " To the evangelical," says R. H. Coats, " the one complete outfit and indispensable *vade mecum* is the Bible " (*op. cit., p.* 86). Old and New Testaments have been read, pondered over and discussed not only in public worship and private meeting, but in the home and the closet. Outward profession has been constantly nurtured by private devotion.

The systematising in the Nonconformist tradition of the more personal side of Puritan devotion may best be studied in the elaborate directions for family and private prayers in Doddridge's *Rise and Progress of Religion in the Human Soul* (1745).[2] The scheme was too elaborate and became artificial and unctuous; nevertheless, it is in itself a refutation of the suggesion that in Protestantism " there has been a tendency to let the spiritual life go by default, and turn to activism and good works." [3] For several generations Doddridge's book was influential among Baptists as well as other Nonconformist groups. The making and renewing of a written personal covenant in the manner enjoined by Doddridge were frequent even in the nineteenth century. The story of how in the 1780s

[2] See E. A. Payne, " The Rise and Progress of Religion in the Soul," *Congregational Quarterly*, XXV. (1947), pp. 9f.

[3] *Catholicity*, 1947, p. 27.

young Samuel Pearce—later the friend of Carey and Fuller—signed such a covenant in his own blood is well-known.[4] There are still in existence a series of statements of religious self-examination and criticism prepared annually by Charles Stovel (1799-1883). The keeping of an intimate religious diary was also a widespread habit. Copious extracts from Fuller's diary will be found in Ryland's memoir of his friend.

Doddridge was read and followed by Baptists. Bunyan was read. The writings of Joseph Alleine and Richard Baxter were still in circulation. The text of Scripture was illuminated for many by Daniel Defoe's *Family Instructor* (1715)—which John Ryland mentions side by side with Bunyan's *Holy War*—by Doddridge's *Family Expositor*, by the commentaries of Matthew Henry and John Gill and, later, by those of the Anglican evangelical, Thomas Scott. Few homes were without one or more of these books. In the early nineteenth century Baptists read J. G. Pike's *Persuasives to Early Piety* (1819) and the *Anxious Enquirer* (1834) of John Angell James. Of the latter 200,000 copies were printed within five years of its publication and the sales had reached half a million before James's death in 1859. R. W. Dale was later to criticise the theological weakness of the *Anxious Enquirer,* but as a youth in his teens he read it on his knees, and in keen distress about his personal salvation. " Night after night," he says, " I waited with eager impatience for the house to become still, that in undisturbed solitude I might agonise over the book which had taught so many to trust in God." [5] C. H. Spurgeon's testimony is very similar. Alleine, Baxter, Doddridge and James were the books he read when he was seeking the light.

[4] See S. Pearce Carey, *Samuel Pearce, the Baptist Brainerd,* p. 66.

[5] A. W. W. Dale, *Life of R. W. Dale,* 1899, p. 16. Cp. pp. 72, 151f.

In the later decades of the nineteenth century it was Spurgeon's own writings which provided spiritual food and instruction for tens of thousands of Nonconformists. His books of daily readings *Morning by Morning* and *Evening by Evening*, provided material for family prayers and personal devotions, and a weekly sermon, sold at a penny, found its way into countless shops, farms and cottages, from which came the majority of Baptist church members and adherents. Spurgeon's writings continued to circulate widely until the first World War and are still in considerable demand on the continent of Europe and in the Dominions. The scripture biographies written by F. B. Meyer (1847-1929) and his books on the spiritual life had also wide influence in Baptist circles and beyond, and there were also the biblical expositions and sermons of Alexander McLaren (1826-1910).

In this as in other realms, however, there were diversities in the Baptist outlook and temperament. Those to whom "methodism" and evangelicalism made little appeal found spiritual and intellectual stimulus in the essays of John Foster (1770-1843). Foster was a Baptist minister, ineffective as preacher and pastor, who as writer gained a remarkable hold over many minds. His most famous essays—" On Decision of Character " and " On Some of the Causes by which Evangelical Religion has been rendered less acceptable to Persons of Cultivated Taste"—first appeared in 1804 and were again and again reprinted. Allusions to them are frequent in nineteenth century biographies. That they long continued effective is shown by the testimony of Dr. John R. Mott to the importance in his own life of Foster's essay " On Decision of Character," read while he was a student at Cornell University in the 1880s. Other influences at work among the few and discriminating, though not the multitude, were the sermons of Edmund Luscombe Hull (1832-62), and the pulpit exercises of S. A. Tipple (1826-1916),

Baptist ministers, the one at King's Lynn and the other at South Norwood. Generations of Baptist candidates for the ministry were trained by men like Joseph Angus and William Medley, who combined a firm hold on evangelical religion with a love of literature and humane studies.

When we turn from the nineteenth century to the twentieth, we find Baptists much more open to influences from other denominations than their own and from other spiritual traditions. Among those, however, who have spoken most effectively to the devotional needs of their day have been two other Baptist ministers, Harry Emerson Fosdick, of New York, and F. W. Boreham, of Australia. Between the two World Wars a wide influence was also exerted by the religious writings of T. R. Glover.

Is there traceable through all this a distinctive pattern of spiritual discipline and piety among Baptists? Not one that is sharply separable from English Puritanism in general, though for the nurturing of their spiritual life Baptists have emphasised certain forms, such as hymns and prayer-meetings, rather more than have other Free Churchmen. Moreover, the rite of believer's baptism in itself involves a constant stress on personal decision and conversion. What has been said in the preceding pages provides evidence of the substantial contribution which Baptists have made to the evangelical tradition, a contribution that has not been confined to their own denomination and one that has not been narrow in conception or merely negative.

Thomas Grantham (1634-92), one of the early General Baptist leaders in Lincolnshire and East Anglia, in his verse dialogue *The Prisoner against the Prelate*, written from Lincoln gaol in 1662, contrasts the worship of the neighbouring Cathedral with that of the imprisoned Baptists :

" And having heard that some in Prison lay,
Because they would not close with that fine way
Of Worship, I therefore anon repaired
To see how these distressed persons fared;
And being come unto their lodging place,
I found the Prisoners, with erected face
To Heaven, with their knees prostrate before
The mighty God, whom They did there adore
With pray'r and praises (which I understood)
And so far fervent, that I gained some good
By this Devotion; for my cogitations
Provoked were to heav'nly meditations
And Christian conference with those distressed,
About the end reserv'd for all the Blessed."

This has always been the aim and intention of Baptist worship and often these things have been achieved. There is a danger, however, that simplicity and freedom may become carelessness and irreverence, and Baptists do not always avoid this danger. The Puritan tradition was a protest against stereotyped forms and elaborations which seemed not only to hinder man's access to God, but to be trivial and almost blasphemous. Those for whom freedom has been won have to beware of like perils. A renewal of the springs of worship, both public and private, is one of the greatest needs of the present age.

Chapter Eight
SOME MODERN ISSUES

I

Our review has been mainly historical, though we have noted a number of important modern pronouncements which indicate the new setting of many of the old problems and certain new issues that have recently emerged. Three outstanding factors in the situation today are, first, the development in extent and authority of the Baptist Union; secondly, the widespread casualness in the local church in regard to what may be roundly described as "churchmanship"; and, thirdly, the general religious situation in this country and, in particular, the changed relationships between different Christian bodies. Each of these points requires some notice.

As we have seen there were proposals even in the seventeenth century for a General Assembly of Baptists. It seemed to many the natural development of that association together of local churches which was regarded as an essential part of their life and witness. Various hindrances prevented anything effective being done. Differences in theology, differences in practice, the fact that many churches were composed of both Baptists and Paedo-baptists, the general situation of Dissenters, the physical difficulties of travel and communication—all presented obstacles to any general union. For a century and a half or more, it was in Associations that the local churches found and expressed their wider interests and fellowship. In the eighteenth century the Baptist Board, at first a Coffee House Society, drew together the ministers of London and neighbourhood, while the Particular Baptist Fund began its long and generous service to ministers and churches in all parts of the country. It was not until the early years of the nineteenth century that the proposal to have some general gathering or organisation was successfully revived.

The Baptist General Union—as it was called—was established in 1813. It was thought of as a society, in an age that loved societies. The founders expressly disclaimed " all manner of superiority and superintendence over the churches; or any authority or power, to impose anything on their faith or practice; their sole intention is to be helpers together " (*Baptist Magazine*, 1813, p. 351). Each year the Union arranged one day's meetings for worship and conference, and for some time it was known as "the denominational meeting." There were no permanent officers. Its declared aims were to increase support for the Baptist Missionary Society and the growing number of Academical Institutions or Colleges for the training of ministers, to foster village preaching, to promote interest in the *Baptist Magazine*, the Particular Baptist Fund and the Widow's Fund, and to consider the establishment of a school for the children of ministers. These were all laudable objects, and they indicate lines of service which it was increasingly clear had to be undertaken on a national rather than a local scale. But the lack of effective organisation prevented anything satisfactory being done at the annual meetings and the General Union languished. In 1831-2 the Baptist Board considered how the work of the Union might be made more useful, and attempts were made to survey the denominational field. Not, however, till 1863, when the Union was reorganised and two yearly general meetings, together with quarterly committee meetings, were agreed upon, can it really be said to have come to life. By then, it should be noted, the Congregational Union, formed in 1831, was well established and had survived its first storms.[1]

[1] See Albert Peel, *These Hundred Years*, 1931.

The Baptist Union slowly but steadily grew in strength during the last three decades of the nineteenth century. It owed much to its first full-time secretary, Samuel Harris Booth. Under his guidance it survived the stresses of the Down-Grade controversy, and drew together the churches of both the General and the Particular Baptist traditions. The real architect of the Union's present position and structure was, however, John Howard Shakespeare, who was appointed secretary in 1898. In the words of T. R. Glover, he " taught all Baptists to form large ideals for their church, to conceive of it as a great society, where differences of tradition should not outweigh the fact of a common faith, and where women should have their function as well as men; to realise it in its world-wide range and significance; and to live more consciously as members one of another." The twenty-six years of Shakespeare's secretariat saw the transformation of the status and authority of the Union. The Baptist Church House was provided as a denominational headquarters in place of two or three rooms at the top of the Baptist Mission House. A large sum was spent by the Union on the building of new chapels, and this was followed by a sustained and successful attempt to organise a denominational scheme of ministerial recognition and sustentation. In passing, it may be noted that it was the Presbyterian system of ministerial appointment and support that was again and again appealed to by the promoters of the scheme. What was done was found to involve the division of the country into a number of areas for administrative purposes and the appointment to each of a minister as " General Superintendent." The rising cost of living during the 1914-18 war compelled the Union, in the carrying out of the new responsibilities it had undertaken, to raise further additional sums of money. The total invested funds of the Union when J. H. Shakespeare became secretary amounted to only

£180,000, of which all but £5,000 belonged to an Annuity Fund. When Shakespeare died in 1926, the invested funds approached £750,000, and the annual income of the Union was more than four times what it had been in 1898. Nor was this all. Through membership of the United Board, the Union had become responsible for the appointment of chaplains to the fighting services; through membership of the Federal Council of the Evangelical Free Churches, it had become the official mouthpiece of all Baptists in their official and general relationships with other Christian bodies. A transformation had taken place in Baptist polity.

The past twenty-five years have seen the further development of the work of the Union and a continued growth in its influence and power. A central Super-annuation Fund for ministers has absorbed the old Annuity Fund and increased its range and benefits. The invested funds of the Union which in 1926 amounted to £750,000 are now in the neighbourhood of £1,250,000. Fresh centralised efforts have been made to encourage church extension. Matters connected with ministerial training and recognition have received increasing attention The Union has itself established an Order of Deaconesses and undertaken their training. As the mouthpiece of Baptists in their relations with other churches, with the Government and with public bodies, the Union has gained almost every year an increase in its prestige and authority. On every side new opportunities of service show themselves.[2]

The development of the Union, among churches with the individualistic traditions of Baptists, has not been easy. To support its day to day work the Union has relied, first of all, on the affiliation fees of churches and Associations, and secondly, on the subscriptions of

[2] On the preceding paragraphs, see E. A. Payne, "The Baptist Union, 1897-1947," *Baptist Quarterly*, XII. (1947), pp., 267f.

personal members who now number some 1,500, and who
may sit in the annual Assembly side by side with the
delegates of the churches. Theoretically, the Union remains a voluntary association of churches, Associations,
colleges and individuals, without what our fathers would
have called "church-power". In practice, it has become
the great centralised organ for the expression of Baptist
churchmanship. It has undertaken with growing efficiency
and success responsibilities which formerly rested upon
local churches or Associations of churches without any
serious facing by Baptists of two important questions :
first, what is involved in all this for the Baptist doctrine
of the church and the ministry; and secondly, are the
constitution of the Union and the way in which its
Council and Committees are elected and function proper
for the exercise of church life and church order?

II

The fifty or sixty years that have witnessed this remarkable growth in a central denominational organisation
have seen also a decline in the strict and responsible
churchmanship of the local congregation. To some extent
the two things are related. Inevitably and rightly, the
local church has had to surrender or delegate certain of
its powers, in order to secure the help of the whole
Baptist community. The denomination as a whole is
clearly entitled, indeed compelled, to satisfy itself as to
the credentials and fitness of those who are to receive
grants in aid, or those who are to be sponsored for public
appointments. It is only right that it should satisfy
itself as to the proper functioning and management of
communities which are to be assisted with a building
subsidy or an annual grant for the maintenance of a
minister. But, as was suggested in the discussion regarding the ministry, far more is involved than efficient
business arrangements.

The local companies of believers have recognised that the representatives of the churches acting together must undertake certain lines of service and they have, whether consciously or unconsciously, gone far to shift the centre of real authority in church matters. " The churches appearing " at a general council or assembly, said the General Baptists in 1678, " make but one church." Increasingly of recent years there has been talk of " the Baptist Church," [3] by which is meant all the Baptist churches conceived as a unit for certain ecclesiastical purposes. Whilst some of this talk has no doubt been careless and ill-considered, yet it does indicate the fact that the conception of the Church has been widened from that of its purely local expression. A local church may at any moment, should it seem right, leave the fellowship of the Baptist Union. It continues to play a very large and essential part in the management of its own affairs, and, in particular, in the calling of a pastor. All church members continue, at least in theory, to share in the government of the church, which in that sense is democratic, and not from above, either by a hierarchy or by a synod. Nevertheless, it has been recognised that the sovereign authority of Christ may be seen and expressed within the ordered life of the whole Baptist community as well as in the local company of believers, and the latter voluntarily accepts certain limitations of and restrictions upon its authority as the price of wider fellowship and more effective service.

The duties which the Baptist pioneers of the seventeenth century laid upon those who formed themselves into

[3] Note the official acceptance of the designation in connection with the work of the War Damage Commission. Dr. Dakin, *op. cit.*, pp. 8, 45 and 47, denies that such language is permissable. The Report on the Church of the Faith and Order Commission preparing for the World Conference of 1952 states (p. 16) : " The modern usage, whereby the denominations are spoken of as the Churches, has no theological justification and is, if a necessity, an evil necessity arising from the anomaly of a divided church."

Christian churches—the choice of church officers, their adequate support, the preaching of the Gospel in the world and the gathering of new companies of believers into a church-state—are now undertaken to an increasing extent by the churches in co-operation with one another. The evidence given in the preceding pages suggests that many of the early Baptist leaders would have been quite ready for this. What they would have asked was that in acting together the true marks and forms of the Church were not lost. It is, however, more important to note that the wider conception of the Church is true to the New Testament.

The word ἐκκλησία has always a universal and unitary as well as a local implication. It is right that Free Churchmen should stress the significance of the frequent appearance of the word in the plural and attached to a particular community of believers in a city, or even in a house. It is also important to insist that in a true sense "the whole mystery of the Church is present in each local part," and that Christ Himself may be in its midst. It is, however, obtuse to ignore the fact that in the New Testament ἐκκλησία is also applied to groups covering a very wide geographical area (e.g. Acts. ix. 31, xx. 28). Further, the great passages in the Pauline correspondence which use the word in the singular of the one Church (e.g. 1 Corinthians xii. 28, Colossians i. 18, 24, Ephesians *passim*, I Timothy iii. 5, 15), together with Matthew xvi. 18 and phrases like "the Body of Christ," "a holy nation," "a peculiar people," etc., which refer to believers corporately, have all application to the church visible, for the later distinction between the Church visible and the Church invisible would not have occurred to the Christians of the first century. K. L. Schmidt is followed by many scholars who have no brief for Roman or High Anglican theories of the Church, in the view that the universal and unitary significance of ἐκκλησία is primary and funda-

mental. " It was one Church in many manifestations;"
said P. T. Forsyth, nearly thirty years ago, " it was not
many churches in one convention " (*The Church and the
Sacraments,* 1917, p. 62 and Chapters II and III *passim*).
Many of our modern developments—within the Baptist
denomination and also in the wider ecumenical movement—are attempts, blundering perhaps, but sincere, to
express in better fashion this New Testament conception
of unity and to get away from the narrowness and
poverty of an exaggerated and degenerate independency.

The Church in this wider sense is, however, made up
of, or expresses its life through, many local churches.
A disturbing factor in the modern situation is the light
way in which the obligations of local church membership
are now often regarded. Our fathers would surely have
questioned whether a community of people could rightly
be described as a church if they had not some kind of
regular pastoral oversight, and if the sacraments, and in
particular the Lord's Supper, were not regularly observed
among them. It is instructive to note how hesitant they
often were to admit companies of believers to separate
existence as " churches." In the closing years of the
eighteenth century, from College Street Church, Northampton, under the leadership of the two Rylands,
regular worship was started in forty or fifty surrounding
villages. Only with considerable reluctance, and with a
very clearly expressed sense of the solemnity of the step
which was being taken, were separate " churches "
formed in the villages. Those at College Street first
sought clear evidence that a proper church-state could
be maintained, that is, that duly qualified church officers
were available, a pastor as well as deacons, and that the
sacraments would be regularly and fitly observed by all
the members, and church discipline properly maintained.[4]

[4] See, e.g. E. A. Payne, *Bugbrooke Baptist Church,* 1930, pp. 7-14,
and Taylor, *The History of College Street, Northampton,* 1897.

We are now prepared to allow the name " churches " to groups of men and women, sometimes extremely small in number, who have no regularly functioning church-meeting, no proper diaconate, no pastor, and among whom the Lord's Supper is only rarely observed. In much larger communities the church has come to be regarded as a kind of voluntary association or society, good in its way, but with its forms not a necessary or essential part of the Christian life. Many even of those who like to have their name on a church roll think so lightly of it that they do not feel it necessarily involves regular attendance at Christian worship.[5] They are not gravely troubled if they fail to be present at the Lord's Table or at the Church-Meeting. It has even become possible for deacons to be lax in these matters.

The widespread opening of membership has resulted in communities of the most mixed ecclesiastical origins and with no strong traditions of their own. Theory and practice in regard to church, ministry and sacraments have in consequence become vague and casual. There may today be many associated with a so-called Baptist church, some even among its deacons and leaders, who are content to remain without the sacrament of baptism. On the other hand, where membership has remained closed to all but baptised believers, the church roll has often little real relationship to the effective life and wit-ness of the fellowship. The most devoted workers as well as the most generous givers may be unable to share in what we are still sometimes told is the really characteristic mark of our type of churchmanship—namely, the selection by the members of their pastor. All kinds of shifts and compromises are sometimes in-

[5] In this regard the situation in the United States, where church membership totals are still rising, is worse than in Britain. See F. C. Stifler, *Better Baptist Churches*, 1937, p. 25 : " Less than two-fifths of our church members are regular worshippers."

dulged in to meet this situation.[6] Further, many who have been baptised on profession of their faith, and who believe that this is clearly the New Testament manner of observing the rite, feel no strong obligation to be in membership with a Baptist church if, on other grounds, such as nearness to their home, or size, or social attractiveness, or general quality of preaching and worship, they are drawn to one of another tradition. It is not very easy to estimate which is the larger number —those who have been Baptists but are now in fellowship with other churches, or those who are associated with Baptist churches but have no convictions regarding what is supposed to be their distinctive witness.

III

We are here brought face to face with the general religious situation in this country. The matters to which attention has been called are not peculiar to Baptists. They affect in one way or another all the branches of the Church, and, as was indicated in our first chapter, they are increasingly the concern of all. There is a general lament that churchmanship is not taken seriously. There is general perplexity in regard to the nature and meaning of the Church. We cannot isolate our problem, or treat it in abstraction from the life of our times.

Baptists are but one of the free Church groups in this country. For more than three hundred years they have shared the fortunes of so-called Protestant Dissenters, those rejecting the national religious settlement—first arranged in the sixteenth century and re-established in 1662—on the ground that they could accept neither uniformity of worship in terms of the Book of Common Prayer, nor episcopacy as the divinely appointed method

[6] That this is no new problem may be seen from a discussion of it in J. D. Humphreys, *Correspondence and Diary of Philip Doddridge,* 1829, Vol. I, p. 313.

of church government. Many, but not all, would add as a further ground of dissent their objection to any nationally-established or state-form of religion. The Free Church tradition has been a long and notable one, and it has made a rich contribution to English life.[7] Its history may be traced from the first protests in the sixteenth century, through the bitter and involved struggles of the seventeenth, to the limited recognition secured in 1689. Next came a sharing in a vast uprush of spiritual power, and an eager evangelism throughout newly industrialised England. Before the Evangelical Revival had entirely spent itself probably half the church-goers of this country were to be found in Nonconformist places of worship. It was impossible any longer to deny to Free Churchmen full civil rights. Throughout the Victorian era they showed increasing strength and confidence and at the beginning of the twentieth century their outlook might be not unfairly taken as " representative of the temper of the English people." [8]

From 1893 when the National Free Church Council was formed, or even earlier, the different Free Churches drew very close together. The things that divided them seemed of minor importance. There was co-operation in practical affairs and mutual borrowing on an extensive scale. Hymns, forms of worship, leadership and scholarship were common to all. A strong anti-ecclesiastical temper was to be found throughout the Free Churches, the product partly of the individualism of the age and partly of conscious reaction from the Oxford Movement. There was far greater interest in the practical application of Christianity than in the visible church either local or in its wider expressions. The natural consequences of these things are to be seen in our present perplexities

[7] See E. A. Payne, *The Free Church Tradition in the Life of England,* 1944.

[8] Cf. D. W. Brogan, *The English People,* 1943, p. 121.

regarding churchmanship. Though the dreams that some have had of a United Free Church have so far failed to be translated into fact, it may well be questioned whether any attempt at a revived segregation of the different Free Church traditions is not now as certain to fail as would be any attempt to return to a pre-Darwinian world-view.

Recent decades have seen increasing hesitancy and loss of confidence on the part of Free Churchmen. Professor Brogan regards " the decline of Nonconformity " as " one of the greatest changes in the English religious and social landscape." It cannot, of course, be considered out of relation to the waning power of organised religion generally, which has been characteristic of the present century. There has been a disintegration of the intellectual, moral and spiritual sanctions which formerly held men and women to the traditional forms of the Christian religion. Not only churchmanship but the faith itself has been challenged. The discoveries of science and the theories based thereon, changed economic conditions and, not least, the shattering effects of two world wars have combined to shake the foundations of all the churches. The Free Churches, based as they have been upon the voluntary principle, have inevitably suffered heavily. There have been many who have felt, with Professor Brogan, " the comparative irrelevance of the peculiarly Nonconformist (as apart from Christian) view of the contemporary world and its problems." We may be quite unprepared to agree to this as a final verdict on our witness, and yet admit how widespread is the acceptance of it at the present time.

For a proper appraisal of the present situation, two further points must be noted. The modern missionary movement has laid the foundations of Christian communities throughout Asia and Africa and in other parts of the world, and there has been a deepening desire to enter into and express Christian fellowship with these " younger " groups, whatever the pattern of their churchmanship. And, further, the Anglican Church, over against which the Free Churches developed their life, has itself profoundly changed. The Lambeth Appeal of 1920 is but one illustration of a new outlook and temper, specially notable because it came from the whole episcopal bench. Of recent years Anglicanism has given a more consistently spiritual lead than ever before in its history. Christian truth and charity are therefore widely felt to demand a much less rigid separation between Christians than characterised the religious history of this and other countries from the sixteenth to the nineteenth centuries. The dispassionate reading of Christian history makes it clear that God has had His servants in all branches of the Church. However strongly the individual or the community may hold to certain principles or practices, these things ought not, so it is increasingly felt, to prevent the clear outward expression of common Christian discipleship.

IV

It is because of this situation that those of many different ecclesiastical traditions are feeling compelled to re-examine the doctrine of the Church. And, of recent days, there is the added incentive that in many lands, east and west, it is the Church which has been the indestructible centre of spiritual resistance to tyranny. The scholars turn again to the study of the New Testament and of Church History.[9] The denominational leaders look once more at the origins and witness of their own communities. The ministers, of whatever church, examine their credentials and authority. Every thoughtful believer is moved to question his own relationship to the Body of Christ and to the channels through which the Holy Spirit has operated and still operates. The widespread spiritual

[9] See Appendix E.

drought has caused many to ask whether among the old wells which could be re-opened that of a more serious churchmanship is not, perchance, one holding at least some of the water of life.

It is a hopeful sign that a new, though wistful, seriousness has come over all Christians in regard to these matters. What is important is that thinking and prayer about the Church and its ministry and sacraments should be both honest and informed. No superficial generalisations will meet our need, no bare repetition of ancient formulæ, no beating of a denominational drum without reference to the notes sounded by other regiments of the Church Militant. " It is simply disastrous," as Dr. Shakespeare reminded us thirty years ago, " when men, wrapped in grave-clothes of dead controversies, utter battle-cries which have lost all their power " (*The Churches at the Cross-Roads*, p. 31). Archaism, as Professor Toynbee has pointed out, is a futile thing. One cannot remount the stream of life.

Nevertheless the past, rightly understood, has much to say to us. Father A. G. Hebert, in a recent book on *The Form of the Church*, remarks : " Probably the greatest of all obstacles in the way of a true reunion is that to a very large extent the original and authentic Free Church traditions have ceased to exist ; the loss of the old-fashioned forms goes hand in hand with a loss of the old Protestant spirit " (p. 121). One does not need to accept Father Hebert's particular application of this, much less the main contentions of his book regarding episcopacy, to realise that there is truth in his words. Elsewhere he remarks that " many Anglican Catholics would bear witness that they have far more living contact and mental sympathy with the neo-Protestant school in the Congregationalist[10] and other Free Churches, than

---

[10] Father Hebert's book is in the nature of a comment on and reply to Mr. D. T. Jenkins's *The Nature of Catholicity*, 1942.

with some fellow Anglicans " (p. 100). This will come as no surprise to those who consider the seriousness with which the early Reformers and the Separatists busied themselves with the true nature of the Church and the forms through which its life should be expressed. Nor will it disturb those who regard " Baptist convictions as a particular form of the consciousness of the Catholic Church " and remember that " catholicity is measured by depth of conviction, not by breadth of opinion " (H. Wheeler Robinson, *The Life and Faith of the Baptists*, 1927, pp. ix-x). Some wise words of the late Dr. Carnegie Simpson should be borne in mind : " A Church has really no business to have ' distinctive ' principles. A Church's principles should be Christian Principles, and if they are Christian principles, then these are not a peculiarity or prerogative of some special communion."

When the first Baptist World Congress met in London in 1905 to form the Baptist World Alliance, at the first main session the Chairman, Dr. Alexander McLaren, declared :—

> " I want no misunderstanding on the part of the English or the American public in regard to the position we occupy in the continuity of the historic Church. I would like as an act of the Congress that there should be an audible and unanimous acknowledgment of our faith. I suggest that, given your consent, it would be an impressive and a right thing, and it would clear away some misunderstanding, if we as a simple acknowledgment rose and repeated the Apostle's Creed."

The suggestion was at once approved and the delegates from Baptist Unions, Conventions and Associations in every continent stood and repeated the ancient baptismal confession of the early church. It was well described at the time as " a historic recitation " (*Baptist Times*,

14 July, 1905). The Baptists of Great Britain, the American Convention, the National Convention, and the Unions of New Zealand, Holland and Denmark are now members of the World Council of Churches. Other Baptist groups are at present outside the Ecumenical Movement, though confessional associations like the Baptist World Alliance are given by the constitution of the World Council their own representation as consultants at meetings of the Assembly and the Central Committee. Whether in membership with the Council or not, Baptists in all parts of the world are increasingly conscious of the need for a fresh examination of their doctrine of the Church and the Sacraments. In preparation for the eighth World Congress at Cleveland (1950), the Baptist World Alliance set up two international Commissions, the one on the doctrine of the Church, the other on the doctrine of Baptism. Both have embarked upon tasks which cannot soon or easily be accomplished.

We have sought in these chapters to set out some of the evidence which must be the special concern of Baptists as they consider their own witness. They, as much as any, need to recover a more serious churchmanship. It is needed in the local fellowship, at public worship, at the Lord's Table and in the church meeting. It is needed also in the councils of the denomination as a whole, and, particularly, in the adaptation of the Baptist Union organisation and machinery to the high responsibilities now placed in its hands. But above all Baptists require a renewed baptism with the spirit of John Smyth, the spirit of the Gainsborough covenant. They possess a birthright of freedom which makes possible change and experimentation. It should make them courageous, adaptable and resilient. They should be able to meet the challenge of the modern world with less difficulty than those for whom traditional practice has great and even sacred authority. In these pages we have seen how deep,

9

wide and strong was the churchmanship of the fathers, and at how many points it may help us in our modern difficulties. But it is the assurance that God has yet more light and truth to break forth out of His Word that should be of most value to us.

Nos decet respondere natalibus nostris. "It behoves us to be worthy of our birth." The words of Cyprian may be applied to our rich historical tradition, but they have an even more pointed reference. The bishop of Carthage was exhorting his friends to be worthy not of their natural birth and inheritance but of their baptism.

THE PARTICULAR BAPTIST CONFESSION
OF 1677

CHAP. XXVI.
Of the Church

[1] Heb. 12
23. Col. 1.
18. Eph.
1. 10, 22,
23, & ch.
5, 23, 27,
32.

1. The Catholick or universal Church, which (with respect to internal work of the Spirit, and truth of grace) may be called invisible, consists of the whole[1] number of the Elect, that have been, are, or shall be gathered into one, under Christ the head thereof; and is the spouse, the body, the fulness of him that filleth all in all.

[2] 1 Cor. 1.
2. Act. 11.
26
[3] Rom. 1.
7. Eph. 1.
20, 21, 22.
[4] 1 Cor.
15. Rev.
2 & ch. 3

2. All persons throughout the world, professing the faith of the Gospel, and obedience unto God by Christ, according unto it; not destroying their own profession by any Errors everting the foundati- [page] on, or unholyness of conversation,[2] are and may be called visible Saints,[3] and of such ought all particular Congregations to be constituted.

[5] Rev. 18.
2. 2 Thes.
2. 11, 12.
[6] Mat. 16.
18. Ps. 72.
17 & Ps.
102. 28.
Rev. 12.
17.

3. The purest Churches under heaven are subject[4] to mixture, and error; and som have so degenerated as to become[5] no Churches of Christ, but Synagogues of Satan; nevertheless Christ always hath had, and ever shall have a[6] Kingdome, in this world, to the end thereof, of such as be-

lieve in him, and make profession
of his Name.

4. The Lord Jesus Christ is the
Head of the Church, in whom by
the appointment of the Father,[7]
all power for the calling, institution, order, or Government of the
Church, is invested in a supream &
soveraigne manner, neither can the
Pope of Rome in any sense be head [page]
thereof, but is[8] that Antichrist,
that Man of sin, and Son of per-
dition, that exaltheth himself in
the Church against Christ, and all
that is called God; whom the
Lord shall destroy with the bright-
ness of his coming.

5. In the execution of his power wherewith he is so intrusted,
the Lord Jesus calleth out of the
World unto himself, through the
Ministry of his word, by his Spirit,[9]
those that are given unto him
by his Father; that they may
walk before him in all the[11]
ways of obedience, which he pre-
scribeth to them in his Word.
Those thus called he commandeth
to walk together in particular societies, or[12] Churches, for their
mutual edification; and the due
performance of that publick worship which he requireth of them
in the World.   [page]

6. The Members of these
Churches are[13] Saints by calling, visibly manifesting and evi-
dencing (in and by their profession and walking) their obedience
unto that call of Christ; and do

[7] Col. 1.
18. Mat.
28, 18, 19,
20.
Eph. 4.
11, 12.
[8] 2 Thes.
2. 3-9.

[9] Joh. 10.
16. chap.
12. 32.
[11] Matt. 28
20.

[12] Mat. 18.
15-20.

[13] Rom. 1.
9. 1 Cor.
1. 2.

willingly consent to walk together according to the appointment of Christ, giving up themselves, to the Lord & one to another by the will of God,[14] in professed subjection to the Ordinances of the Gospel.

7. To each of these Churches thus gathered, according to his mind, declared in his word, he hath given all that[15] power and authority, which is any way needfull, for their carrying on that order in worship, and discipline, which he hath instituted for them to observe; with commands, and rules for the due and right exerting, and executing of that power.

8. A particular Church gathered, and compleatly Organized, according to the mind of Christ, consists of Officers, and Members; And the Officers appointed by *Christ* to be chosen and set apart by the Church (so called and gathered) for the peculiar Administration of Ordinances, and Execution of Power, or Duty, which he intrusts them with, or calls them to, to be continued to the end of the World, or[16] Bishops or Elders and Deacons.

9. The way appointed by *Christ* for the Calling of any person, fitted, and gifted by the Holy *Spirit,* unto the Office of Bishop, or Elder, in a Church, is, that he be chosen thereunto by the common[17] suffrage of the Church it self; and Solemnly set apart by

[14] Act. 2. 41, 42. ch. 5. 13, 14. 2 Cor. 9. 13.

[15] Mat. 18. 17, 18. 1 Cor. 5. 4, 5, with 5. 13

[16] Act. 20. 17, with v. 28. Phil. 1. 1.

[17] Act. 14. 23. See the original.

[18] 1 Tim. 4. 14.

Fasting and Prayer, with imposition of hands of the[18] Eldership of the Church, if there be any before [page] Constituted therein; And of a Deacon[19] that he be chosen by the like suffrage, and set apart by Prayer, and the like Imposition of hands.

[19] Act. 6. 3, 5, 6.

10. The work of Pastors being to attend the Service of *Christ,* in his Churches, in the Ministry of the Word, and Prayer,[20] with watching for their Souls, as they that must give an account to him; it is incumbent on the Churches to whom they Minister, not only to give them all due respect,[21] but also to communicate to them of all their good things according to their ability, so as they may have a comfortable supply, without being themselves[24] entangled in Secular Affairs; and may also be capable of exercising[25] Hospitality towards others; and this is required by the[26] Law of Nature, and by the Express order of our [page] Lord Jesus, who hath ordained that they that preach the Gospel, should live of the Gospel.

[20] Act. 6. 4. Heb. 13. 17.

[21] 1 Tim. 5. 17, 18. Gal. 6. 6. 7.

[24] 2 Tim. 2. 4.

[25] 1 Tim. 3. 2.

[26] 1 Cor. 9. 6-14.

11. Although it be incumbent on the Bishops or Pastors of the Churches to be instant in Preaching the Word, by way of Office; yet the work of Preaching the Word, is not so peculiarly confined to them; but that others also[1] gifted, and fitted by the Holy *Spirit* for it, and approved, and

[1] Act. 11. 19, 20, 21. 1 Pet. 4. 10, 11.

called by the *Church,* may and
ought to perform it.

12. As all Believers are bound
to joyn themselves to particular
Churches, when and where they
have opportunity so to do; So all
that are admitted unto the privi-
ledges of a *Church,* are also[2]
under the Censures and Government thereof, according to the
Rule of *Christ.*   [page]

13. No Church-members upon
any offence taken by them, having performed their Duty required
of them towards the person they
are offended at, ought to disturb
any *Church* order, or absent themselves from the Assemblies of the
Church, or Administration of any
Ordinances, upon the account of
such offence at any of their fellow-
members; but to wait upon *Christ,*[3]
in the further proceeding of the
Church.

14. As each *Church,* and all the
Members of it, are bound to[4]
pray continually, for the good
and prosperity of all the *Churches* of
Christ, in all places; and upon
all occasions to further it (every
one within the bounds of their
places, and callings, in the Exercise of their Gifts and Graces) so
the *Churches* (when planted by
the providence of God so as they
may injoy opportunity and advantage for it) ought to hold[5]   [page]
communion amongst them-
selves for their peace, increase of
love, and mutual edification.

[2] 1 Thess.
5. 14
2 Thes. 3.
6, 14, 15.

[3] Mat. 18.
15, 16, 17.
Eph. 4. 2,
3.
[4] Eph. 6.
18. Ps.
122. 6.

[5] Rom.
16. 1, 2.
3 Joh. 8,
9, 10.

15. In cases of difficulties or differences, either in point of Doctrine, or Administration; wherein either the Churches in general are concerned, or any one Church in their peace, union, and edification; or any member, or members, of any Church are injured, in or by any proceedings in censures not agreeable to truth, and order; it is according to the mind of Christ, that many Churches holding communion together, do by their messengers meet to consider,[6] and give their advice in, or about that matter in difference, to be reported to all the Churches concerned; howbeit these messengers assembled, are not entrusted with any Church-power properly so called; or with any jurisdiction over the Churches themselves, to exercise any censures either over any [page] Churches, or Persons: or[7] to impose their determination on the Churches, or Officers.

[6] Act. 15. 2, 4, 6. & 22, 23, 25.

[7] 2 Cor. 1. 24. 1 Joh. 4. 1

CHAP. XXVII.

On the Communion of Saints.

[1] 1 Joh. 1. 3. Joh. 1. 16. Phil 3. 10 Rom. 6. 5, 6.

1. All *Saints* that are united to Jesus Christ their *Head,* by his Spirit, and Faith; although they are not made thereby one person with him, have[1] fellowship in his Graces, sufferings,

death, resurrection, and glory;
and being united to one another
in love, they[2] have communion
in each others gifts, and graces;
and obliged to the performance of such duties, publick and
private, in an orderly way,[3] as
do conduce to their mutual good,
both in the inward and outward
man.

[page]

2. *Saints* by profession are
bound to maintain an holy fellowship and communion in the
worship of God, and in perform-
ing such other spiritual services,[4]
as tend to their mutual edification; as also in relieving each
other in[5] outward things according to their several abilities,
and necessities; which communion, according to the rule of the
Gospel, though especially to be exercised by them, in the relations
wherein they stand, whether in[6]
families, or[7] Churches;
yet as God offereth opportunity
is to be extended to all the hous-
hold of faith, even all those who
in every place call upon the name
of the Lord Jesus; nevertheless
their communion one with another as *Saints,* doth not take away
or[8] infringe the title or pro-
priety, which each man hath in his
goods and possessions. [page]

[2] Eph. 4
15, 16.
1 Cor. 12.
7 1 Cor.
3. 21,
22, 23.

[3] 1 Thes.
5. 11, 14.
Rom. 1.
12. 1 Joh.
2. 17, 18.
Gal. 6, 10.

[4] Heb. 10.
24, 25
with ch.
3. 12, 13.

[5] Act. 12.
29, 30.

[6] Eph. 6.
4.

[7] 1 Cor.
12. 14.
27.

[8] Act. 5. 4.
Eph. 4
28.

CHAP. XXVIII.

Of Baptism and the Lords Supper.

1. Baptism and the Lord's Supper are ordinances of positive, and soveraign institution; appointed by the Lord Jesus the only Law-giver, to be continued in his Church[1] to the end of the world.

2. These holy appointments are to be administered by those only, who are qualified and thereunto called according[2] to the commission of Christ. [page]

[1] Mat. 28. 19, 20. 1 Cor. 11. 26.

[2] Mat. 28. 19. 1 Cor. 4. 1.

CHAP. XXIX.

Of Baptism.

1. Baptism is an Ordinance of the New Testament, ordained by Jesus Christ, to be unto the party Baptized, a sign of his fellowship with him, in his death,[3] and resurrection; of his being engrafted into him; of[4] remission of sins; and of his[5] giving up unto God through Jesus Christ, to live and walk in newness of Life.

2. Those who do actually profess[6] repentance towards *God,* faith in, and obedience, to our Lord Jesus, are the only proper subjects of this ordinance. [page]

3. The outward element to be

[3] Rom. 6. 3, 4, 5. Col. 2. 12. Gal. 3. 27.

[4] Mar. 1. 4. Act. 26. 16.

[5] Rom. 6. 2, 4.

[6] Mar. 16. 16. Act. 8. 36, 37.

[7] Mat. 28.
19, 20,
with Act
8. 38.

used in this ordinance[7] is water, wherein the party is to be baptized, in the name of the Father, and of the Son, and of the Holy Spirit.

4. Immersion, or dipping of the person[8] in water, is necessary to the due administration of this ordinance.

[8] Mat. 3.
16. Joh. 3.
23.

CHAP. XXX.

Of the Lords Supper.

1. The Supper of the Lord Jesus, was instituted by him, the same night wherein he was betrayed, to be observed in his Churches unto the end of the [page] world, for the perpetual remembrance, and shewing forth the sacrifice in his death[1]

[1] 1 Cor.
11. 23, 24,
25, 26.

confirmation of the faith of believers in all the benefits thereof, their spiritual nourishment, and growth in him, their further ingagement in, and to, all duties which they owe unto him;[2]

[2] 1 Cor.
10. 16, 17,
21.

and to be a bond and pledge of their communion with him, and with each other.

2. In this ordinance Christ is not offered up to his Father, nor any real sacrifice made at all, for remission of sin of the quick or dead; but only a memorial of that[3] one offering up of himself, by himself, upon the crosse, once for

[3] Heb. 9.
25, 26. 28.

[4] 1 Cor.
11. 24.
Mat. 26.
26, 27.

all; and a spiritual oblation of all[4] possible praise unto God for the same; so that the Popish sacrifice of the Mass (as they call it) is most obominable, injurous to Christs own only sacrifice, the [page] alone propitiation for all the sins of the Elect.

3. The Lord Jesus hath in this Ordinance, appointed his Ministers to Pray, and bless the Elements of Bread and Wine, and thereby to set them apart from a common to an holy use, and to take and break the Bread; to take the Cup,[5] and (they communicating also themselves) to give both to the Communicants.

[5] 1 Cor.
11, 23, 24,
25, 26, etc.

4. the denyal of the Cup to the people, worshipping the Elements, the lifting them up, or carrying them about for adoration, and reserving them for any pretended religious use,[6] are all contrary to the nature of this Ordinance, and to the institution of Christ.

[6] Mat. 26.
26, 27, 28.
Mat. 15. 9.
Exod. 20.
4, 5.

5. The outward Elements in this Ordinance, duely set apart to [page] the uses ordained by Christ, have such relation to him crucified, as that truely, although in terms used figuratively, they are sometimes called by the name of the things they represent, to wit[7] body and Blood of Christ; albeit in substance, and nature, they still remain truly, and only[8] Bread, and Wine, as they were before.

[7] 1 Cor.
11. 27.
[8] 1 Cor.
11. 26 &
5. 28.

6. That doctrine which main-

tains a change of the substance of
Bread and Wine, into the substance
of Christ's body and blood (commonly called Transubtantiation)
by consecration of a Priest, or by
any other way, is repugnant not to

[9] Act. 3.
21. Luk.
24. 6 & 5.
39.

Scripture[9] alone, but even to
common sense and reason; overthroweth

[11] 1 Cor.
11, 24, 25.

the[11] nature of the or-
dinance, and hath been and is the
cause of manifold superstitions, yea, of gross
Idolatries.   [page]

7. Worthy receivers, outwardly partaking of the visible Elements in this Ordinance, do then
also inwardly by faith, really and
indeed, yet not carnally, and corporally, but spiritually receive,

[12] 1 Cor.
10. 16. ch.
11. 23.
26.

and feed upon Christ crucified[12] &
all the benefits of his death: the
Body and Blood of *Christ,* being
then not corporally, or carnally,
but spiritually present to the faith
of Believers, in that Ordinance, as
the Elements themselves are to
their outward senses.

8. All ignorant and ungodly
persons, as they are unfit to enjoy

[13] 2 Cor.
6. 14, 15.

communion[13] with *Christ;* so
are they unworthy of the Lords
Table; and cannot without great
sin against him, while they remain
such, partake of these holy myste-

[14] 1 Cor.
11. 29.
Mat. 7. 6.

ries,[14] or be admitted thereunto: yea whosoever shall receive
unworthily are guilty of the Body and Blood of the Lord, eating
and drinking judgment to them-
selves.   [page]

THE BAPTIST REPLY TO THE LAMBETH APPEAL, ADOPTED BY THE ANNUAL ASSEMBLY, MAY 4, 1926

We the representatives of Churches in membership with the Baptist Union of Great Britain and Ireland, gathered in Annual Assembly, greet in the name of our Lord Jesus Christ all Christian people, and at this time especially those within the Anglican Church.

The " Appeal to All Christian People," issued by the Lambeth Conference of 1920, and transmitted to us by the Archbishop of Canterbury, has stirred deeply our minds and hearts. We received it with the respect and sympathy due to a message from brethren in Christ representing a great historic communion and moved by a spirit of brotherly love towards their fellow Christians; and we have sought to give it the prayerful consideration which it manifestly deserves.

Our reply has been postponed in order that the Federal Council of the Free Churches of England might report upon conversations held with representative Anglican Bishops for the purpose of elucidating the Appeal and the Resolutions that, in the Report of the Lambeth Conference, accompanied it. These conversations having been suspended, and certain documents having been issued by the Joint Conference of Bishops and members of the Federal Council, we are now able to present our reply.

We recognise fully and gladly the courtesy and lofty purpose of those who made the Appeal. These qualities are manifest not only in the document itself, but also in the attitude of their representatives throughout the discussion of the high matters which they brought before us.   We associate ourselves with our Anglican brethren in longing and prayer for a larger unity among all who follow and serve our Lord and Saviour Jesus Christ. While we cannot recall without thankfulness and pride the loyalty to truth which constrained our spiritual ancestors to form the Churches of our faith and order, we sorrow sincerely for whatever has been unworthy in the relations of Christian communities to one another ; and we express our repentance for any bitter or unjust word or deed through which we may have obscured the testimony of the Gospel or hindered the advance of the Kingdom of God.

We believe in the Catholic Church as the holy society of believers in our Lord Jesus Christ, which He founded, of which He is the only Head, and in which He dwells by His Spirit, so that though made up of many communions, organised in various modes, and scattered throughout the world, it is yet one in Him.

We believe that this holy society is truly to be found wherever companies of believers unite as Churches on the ground of a confession of personal faith.   Every local community thus constituted is regarded by us as both enabled and responsible for self-government through His indwelling Spirit who supplies wisdom, love, and power, and who, as we believe, leads these communities to associate freely in wider organisations for fellowship and the propagation of the Gospel.

We reverence and obey the Lord Jesus Christ, our God and Saviour, as the sole and absolute authority in all matters pertaining to faith and practice, as revealed in the Scriptures, and we hold that each Church has liberty to interpret and administer His laws.   We do not judge the conscience of those who take another view, but we believe that this principle of the freedom of the individual Church under Christ has the sanction of Scripture and the justification of history, and therefore we cannot abandon it without being false to our trust. Moreover, it is plain to us that the headship and sole authority of our Lord in His Church excludes any such relations with the State as may impair its liberty.

This view of the church determines our attitude towards the special issues raised by the Lambeth Appeal.

The Scriptures, in and through which the Spirit of God speaks possess for us supreme and unique authority. While we recognize the historic value of ancient creeds, we cannot give them a place of authority comparable with that of the Scriptures.

Christian Baptism and the Communion of the Lord's Supper are duly received by us not only as rites instituted and hallowed by our Lord Himself but as means of grace to all who receive them in faith.

Because we hold the Church to be a community of Christian believers, the ordinance of baptism is administered among us to those only who make a personal confession of repentance and faith. We baptise by immersion in water in accordance with the mode of baptism received by our Lord and practised by His earliest followers as recorded in the New Testament, and because this symbolic representation guards the thought of that inner baptism of the Holy Spirit which is central in Christian experience. In our judgment the baptism of infants incapable of offering a personal confession of faith subverts the conception of the Church as the fellowship of believers. We recognise that those concerning whom Jesus said " Of such is the kingdom of heaven " belong to God, and believe that no rite is needed to bring them into relation with Him. But many of our Churches hold services at which infants are presented, the duties, privileges, and responsibilities of parents emphasized, and the prayers of the Church offered for children and parents.

The Lord's Supper is observed regularly and devoutly by our Churches. Its value for us depends upon both the presence of our Lord and the faith with which we receive the bread and wine that show forth His redemptive sacrifice; but not upon the official position of a celebrant or upon any change in the elements due to words of consecration. It seems to us contrary to the simplicity that is in Christ that the full effect of the Lord's Supper as a means of grace should be held to depend on episcopal ordination.

In general, the place given to Sacraments by the Lambeth Appeal would, it appears, exclude from the universal Church of our Lord bodies of devoted Christians with whom we enjoy fellowship, and to this exclusion we cannot assent.

Our doctrine of the Church determines our conception of the ministry. We hold firmly the priesthood of all believers, and therefore have no separated order of priests. The ministry is for us a gift of the Spirit to the Church, and is an office involving both the inward call of God and the commission of the Church. We can discover no ground for believing that such commission can be given only through an episcopate, and we hold that the individual Church is competent to confer it. For us there is no more exalted office than a ministry charged with preaching the Word of God and with the care of souls. Those called to devote their whole lives to such tasks are held in special honour. Yet any full description of the ministerial functions exercised among us must also take account of other believers who, at the call of the Church, may preside at the observance of the Lord's Supper or fulfil any other duties which the Church assigns to them.

Our ministry is one of those which our brethren of the Anglican Church cordially recognise in their Appeal as having been "manifestly blessed and owned by the Holy Spirit as effective means of grace." Since God has used it in building up Baptist Churches throughout the world which now comprise more than eleven million communicants, we cannot in any way deny its validity and sufficiency.

The deepening sense of friendship and unity between the various parts of the one Church of Christ gladdens us. We thank God that many ancient misunderstandings are passing away, that in our own country hostility and bitterness are giving place to charity and co-operation, and that the Lambeth Appeal by its language and spirit has drawn the churches nearer to one another.

It will be gathered from this reply that union of such a kind as the Bishops have contemplated is not possible for us. We would say this not only with that frankness which we believe is the highest courtesy among Christian brethren, but with the assurance of our regret that the way in which they would have us go with them is not open.

Further progress in the direction of Christian unity can be secured, we are convinced, only by unreserved mutual recognition. We gladly acknowledge the reality of the ministry of our Anglican brethren, whose representative Bishops have similarly acknowledged the reality of our ministry. This mutual recognition is significant and full of hope.

We believe that the time has come when the Churches of Christ should unite their forces to meet the need of the world. We therefore are prepared to join the Church of England in exploring the possibility of a federation of equal and autonomous Churches in which the several parts of the Church of Christ would co-operate in bringing before men the will and the claims of our Lord.

We assure our brethren of our earnest prayer that the blessing of God may rest upon the Churches of the

Anglican Communion, and that He may continuue to im-
part abundantly to its members the riches of His grace.

Finally, we would reaffirm our belief in the real
spiritual unity of all who are loyal to Christ and His
truth, and our eagerness to welcome every means by
which, in common action for the spread of His message
and the helping and healing of men, that unity may be
displayed to the world.

Grace be with all them that love our Lord Jesus Christ
in sincerity.

"CHRISTIAN REUNION."

Reply of the Council of the Baptist Union of Great Britain and Ireland to the letter of the Federal Council of the Evangelical Free Churches, conveying the three documents which had been issued for the consideration of the Churches by a Joint Committee of Anglicans and Free Churchmen.

The Council of the Baptist Union of Great Britain and Ireland acknowledge the receipt of the three documents remitted to it, viz., "Outline of a Reunion Scheme," "The Practice of Inter-Communion," and "1662 and Today." These have received careful consideration. The Council desire, at the outset, to express to the Federal Council of Evangelical Free Churches and, through this, to the Joint Conference of Anglicans and Free Churchmen, their appreciation of the evident desire in putting forward these proposals to do justice to the convictions of all who are concerned, and the patient care shown in the consideration of particular problems. They wish to express their own deep desire to promote a closer fellowship of all believers in Christ and the more effective work and witness of the whole Church of Christ. All that is here said is said in the spirit of that desire and in the confidence that it can be furthered only by brotherly regard, mutual respect for deeply held convictions, and Christian frankness.

It is therefore with profound regret that the members of the Council of the Baptist Union are compelled to say that they cannot regard the "Outline of a Reunion Scheme" as affording a basis for organic reunion. Their chief grounds for this decision are already contained or implied in their reply (1926) to the Lambeth " Appeal " of 1920, but may here be briefly recapitulated.

(1) They hold that Baptism, in the New Testament period, was Baptism by immersion and administered only to believers, and they are unable to accept the subsequent extension of the rite to infants in the practice of the Church. This inability is due, not only to the absence of any New Testament authority for this extension, but still more to the conviction that the essential meaning and value of Baptism according to the New Testament are changed or obscured when it is administered to those who necessarily lack the cardinal requirements of repentance and faith. Only when these requirements are fulfilled is it possible for Baptists to recognise in Baptism a divinely appointed " means of grace " for the baptised person. But when they are fulfilled (as in the Baptism of believers) the rite becomes a true sacrament, in which the believer, obeying the ordinance of God, receives from God in response to his faith, a fuller measure of the Holy Spirit. Because Baptists regard the Church as a fellowship of believers they cannot recognise Infant Baptism as an alternative form of admission into " the united Church of England." Their conviction is that the same condition is required by the New Testament for Baptism as for the attainment of communicant status, viz., personal faith, and that only by fidelity to this condition can the true character of the Church as the fellowship of believers be adequately maintained.

(2) They do not regard the congregational form of Church government, practised by themselves, as essential to the constitution of the Church, though they believe that it does, in many respects, express important elements in the life of the truly Christian society. They are prepared to consider any change of order in Baptist Church polity which would increase the efficiency of the

Church by helping to make it a truer fellowship of the Holy Spirit. But they are unable to take for granted an episcopal form of government, simply on the ground of its large place in the history of the Church, nor do they think that an acknowledged ambiguity in the meaning of " episcopal ordination " would provide a sure foundation for organic union. (The reference is to the statement, on page 15 of the " Outline," that the proposed acceptance of episcopal ordination " neither affirms nor excludes the view that Apostolic Succession determines the validity of the Ministry and Sacraments.")

(3) They believe that it is in accordance with the will of God and in the truest interests of the Church that individual Christians, men or women, having the suitable gifts, should be solemnly set apart by the Church as its ministers; in many cases this is done by the Apostolic practice of prayer and the laying on of hands by recognised representatives of the Church. But they do not believe that such ordination confers a priesthood other than that already possessed by all believers, and they regard as fully valid the ministry of any Christian, man or woman, whom the Christian community may invite to preach, to administer the sacraments, or to discharge any other ministerial duty. In all these cardinal points of dissent from the proposals of the " Outline," they believe that they express the convictions, not of themselves alone, but of the twelve million Baptist communicants with whom they are in fellowship throughout the world. Even if their own convictions did not make it impossible for them to consider organic union on the lines suggested, they would shrink from introducing schism into this great Christian Church of many lands, races and tongues.

In conclusion they would recall the statement made in 1926, that they are ready to explore " the possibility of a federation of equal and autonomous Churches in which the several parts of the Church of Christ would co-operate in bringing before man the will and claims of our Lord." The Council desires to reaffirm this statement, with an increased sense of its importance and urgency, in view of the present world-situation. They recognise the value of intercourse and discussion amongst Christians of the different Churches in which they desire to share for the promotion of mutual understanding of firmly held beliefs which is the necessary condition of fruitful co-operation. They believe that increased loyalty to such convictions on the part of all, coupled with the willingness to learn from each other and to be ready at all times to test convictions by the authority of revelation, will bring all the Churches nearer together and nearer to the will of their common Lord and Saviour, Jesus Christ.

November, 1938.

Appendix D

THE BAPTIST DOCTRINE OF THE CHURCH

A Statement approved by the Council of the Baptist Union of Great Britain and Ireland, March, 1948.

(1) The Baptist Union of Great Britain and Ireland represents more than three thousand churches and about three hundred thousand members. Through its membership in the Baptist World Alliance it is in fellowship with other Baptist communities throughout the world numbering about thirteen million, who have accepted the responsibilities of full communicant membership.

Baptists have a continuous history in Great Britain since the beginning of the seventeenth century. Many of their principles, however, were explicitly proclaimed in the second half of the sixteenth century by the radical wing of the Reformation movement. They claim as their heritage also the great central stream of Christian doctrine and piety through the centuries, and have continuity with the New Testament Church in that they rejoice to believe and seek faithfully to proclaim the Apostolic Gospel and endeavour to build up the life of their churches after what seems to them the New Testament pattern.

The One Holy Catholic Church

(2) Although Baptists have for so long held a position separate from that of other communions, they have always claimed to be part of the one holy catholic Church of our Lord Jesus Christ. They believe in the catholic Church as the holy society of believers in our Lord Jesus Christ, which He founded, of which He is the only Head, and in which He dwells by His Spirit, so that though manifested in many communions, organised in various modes, and scattered throughout the world, it is yet one

in Him.[1] The Church is the Body of Christ and a chosen instrument of the divine purpose in history.

In the worship, fellowship and witness of the one Church we know ourselves to be united in the communion of saints, not only with all believers upon earth, but also with those who have entered into life everlasting.

The origin of the Church is in the Gospel—in the mighty acts of God, the Incarnation, Ministry, Death, Resurrection and Ascension of our Lord and the Descent of the Holy Spirit. Thus it is the power of God in Christ which created the Church and which sustains it through the centuries. It is historically significant that Christ, at the outset of His ministry, " chose twelve to be with Him " and gathered His people into a new community. In our judgment there is no evidence in the New Testament to show that He formally organised the Church, but He did create it. This " New Israel," the expansion of which is recorded in the *Acts of the Apostles* and the *Epistles,* is the heir to the " Old Israel," yet it is marked by vital and significant differences. It is based upon the New Covenant; membership is not constituted by racial origins, but by a personal allegiance; the ritual of temple and synagogue has given place to the ordinances of the Gospel and the national consciousness has widened to world horizons. The Messianic community was reborn by the events of the Gospel and is " a new creation." Therefore, whilst there is an historical continuity with the Old Israel, Old Testament analogies do not determine the character and structure of the New Testament Church.

THE STRUCTURE OF LOCAL BAPTIST CHURCHES

(3) (*a*) It is in membership of a local church in one place that the fellowship of the one holy catholic Church

[1] See reply of the Baptist Union Annual Assembly to the Lambeth Conference Appeal to all Christian People, May 4th, 1926.

becomes significant. Indeed, such gathered companies of believers are the local manifestation of the one Church of God on earth and in heaven. Thus the church at Ephesus is described, in words which strictly belong to the whole catholic Church, as " the church of God, which He hath purchased with His own blood " (Acts xx. 28). The vital relationship to Christ which is implied in full communicant membership in a local church carries with it membership in the Church which is both in time and in eternity, both militant and triumphant. To worship and serve in such a local Christian community is, for Baptists, of the essence of Churchmanship.

Such churches are gathered by the will of Christ and live by the indwelling of His Spirit. They do not have their origin, primarily, in human resolution. Thus the Baptist Confession of 1677,[2] which deals at length with doctrine and church order, uses phrases which indicate that local churches are formed by the response of believing men to the Lord's command. Out of many such phrases we may quote the following : " Therefore they do willingly consent to walk together according to the appointment of Christ." Churches are gathered " according to His mind, declared in His word." Membership was not regarded as a private option, for the *Confession* continues : " All believers are bound to join themselves to particuuar churches when and where they have opportunity so to do." In our tradition discipleship involves both church membership and a full acceptance of the idea of churchmanship.

(*b*) The basis of our membership in the church is a conscious and deliberate acceptance of Christ as Saviour and Lord by each individual. There is, we hold, a personal crisis in the soul's life when a man stands alone in God's presence, responds to God's gracious activity, accepts His forgiveness and commits himself to the

[2] W. J. McGothlin, Baptist Confessions of Faith, p. 265f.

Christian way of life. Such a crisis may be swift and emotional or slow-developing and undramatic, and is normally experienced within and because of our life in the Christian community, but it is always a personal experience wherein God offers His salvation in Christ, and the individual, responding by faith, receives the assurance of the Spirit that by grace he is the child of God. It is this vital evangelical experience which underlies the Baptist conception of the Church and is both expressed and safeguarded by the sacrament of Believers' Baptism.

(c) The life of a gathered Baptist church centres in worship, in the preaching of the Word, in the observance of the two sacraments of Believers' Baptism and the Lord's Supper, in growth in fellowship and in witness and service to the world outside. Our forms of worship are in the reformed tradition and are not generally regulated by liturgical forms. Our tradition is one of spontaneity and freedom, but we hold that there should be disciplined preparation of every part of the service. The sermon, as an exposition of the Word of God and a means of building up the faith and life of the congregation, has a central place in public worship. The Scriptures are held by us to be the primary authority both for the individual in his belief and way of life and for the Church in its teaching and modes of government. It is the objective revelation given in scripture which is the safeguard against a purely subjective authority in religion. We firmly hold that each man must search the Scriptures for himself and seek the illumination of the Holy Spirit to interpret them. We know also that Church history and Christian experience through the centuries are a guide to the meaning of scripture. Above all. we hold that the eternal Gospel—the life, death and resurrection of our Lord—is the fixed point from which our interpretation, both of the Old and New Testaments, and of later developments in the Church, must proceed.

The worship, preaching, sacramental observances, fellowship and witness are all congregational acts of the whole church in which each member shares responsibility, for all are held to be of equal standing in Christ, though there is a diversity of gifts and a difference of functions. This responsibility and this equality are focused in the church meeting which, under Christ, cares for the well-being of the believing community and appoints its officers. It is the responsibility of each member, according to his gifts, to build up the life of his brother and to maintain the spiritual health of the church (Rom. xv. 14). It is the church meeting which takes the responsibility of exercising that discipline whereby the church withdraws from members who are unruly and have ceased to share in her convictions and life.

The church meeting, though outwardly a democratic way of ordering the affairs of the church, has deeper significance. It is the occasion when, as individuals and as a community, we submit ourselves to the guidance of the Holy Spirit and stand under the judgments of God that we may know what is the mind of Christ. We believe that the structure of local churches just described springs from the Gospel and best preserves its essential features.

(d) The Christian doctrine of the Trinity asserts a relationship of Persons within the Godhead, and God has revealed Himself in the Person of His Son, our Saviour Jesus Christ. Thus the Gospel is the basis of the Christian evaluation of men and women as persons. Behind the idea of the gathered church lies the profound conviction of the importance of each man's growth to spiritual maturity and of the responsibility which, as a member of the divine family, he should constantly exercise.

(e) Although each local church is held to be competent, under Christ, to rule its own life, Baptists, throughout their history, have been aware of the perils of isolation and have sought safeguards against exaggerated individualism. From the seventeenth century there have been " Associations " of Baptist churches which sometimes appointed Messengers; more recently, their fellowship with one another has been greatly strengthened by the Baptist Union, the Baptist Missionary Society and the Baptist World Alliance. In recent years, General Superintendents have been appointed by the Baptist Union to have the care of churches in different areas. Indeed, we believe that a local church lacks one of the marks of a truly Christian community if it does not seek the fellowship of other Baptist churches, does not seek a true relationship with Christians and churches of other communions and is not conscious of its place in the one catholic Church. To quote again from the Confession of 1677 :—

> " As each church and all the members of it are bound to pray continually for the good and prosperity of all the churches of Christ in all places; and upon occasions to further it . . . so the churches . . . ought to hold communion amongst themselves for their peace, increase of love and mutual edification."

The Ministry

(4) A properly ordered Baptist church will have its duly appointed officers. These will include the minister (or pastor), elders, deacons, Sunday school teachers and other church workers. The Baptist conception of the ministry is governed by the principle that it is a ministry of a church and not only a ministry of an individual. It is the church which preaches the Word and celebrates the sacraments, and it is the church which, through pastoral oversight, feeds the flock and ministers to the world. It normally does these things through the person

of its minister, but not solely through him. Any member of the church may be authorised by it, on occasion, to exercise the functions of the ministry, in accordance with the principle of the priesthood of all believers, to preach the Word, to administer baptism, to preside at the Lord's table, to visit, and comfort or rebuke members of the fellowship.

Baptists, however, have had from the beginning an exalted conception of the office of the Christian minister and have taken care to call men to serve as pastors. The minister's authority to exercise his office comes from the call of God in his personal experience, but this call is tested and approved by the church of which he is a member and (as is increasingly the rule) by the representatives of a large group of churches. He receives intellectual and spiritual training and is then invited to exercise his gift in a particular sphere. His authority, therefore, is from Christ through the believing community. It is not derived from a chain of bishops held to be lineally descended from the Apostles, and we gratefully affirm that to our non-episcopal communities, as to those episcopally governed, the gifts of the Spirit and the power of God are freely given.

Many among us hold that since the ministry is the gift of God to the Church and the call to exercise the functions of a minister comes from Him, a man who is so called is not only the minister of a local Baptist church, but also a minister of the whole Church of Jesus Christ.

Ordination takes place when a man has satisfactorily completed his college training and has been called to the pastorate of a local church, appointed to a chaplaincy service or accepted for service abroad by the Committee of the Baptist Missionary Society. The ordination service is presided over by either the Principal of his college, a General Superintendent or a senior minister and is shared in by other ministers and lay representatives of the church. Though there is no prescribed or set form of service, it invariably includes either a personal statement of faith or answers to a series of questions regarding the faith. From the seventeenth century onwards, ordination took place with the laying on of hands : in the nineteenth century this custom fell into disuse, but is now again increasingly practised.

The Sacraments

(5) In the preceding sections we have sought to describe the life and ministry of Baptist churches. It is in their total activity of worship and prayer, sacrament and service that the grace of God is continuously given to believing men and women.

We recognise the two sacraments of Believers' Baptism and the Lord's Supper as being of the Lord's ordaining. We hold that both are "means of grace" to those who receive them in faith, and that Christ is really and truly present, not in the material elements, but in the heart and mind and soul of the believer and in the Christian community which observes the sacrament. Our confidence in this rests upon the promises of Christ and not upon any power bestowed on the celebrant in virtue of ordination or succession in ministry. We believe it is important not to isolate the sacraments from the whole action of divine grace, but to see them always in the context of the total activity of the worshipping, believing and serving fellowship of the church.

Following the guidance of the New Testament we administer Baptism only to those who have made a responsible and credible profession of " repentance towards God and faith in the Lord Jesus Christ." Such persons are then immersed in the name of the Father, the Son and the Holy Spirit. Salvation is the work of God in Christ, which becomes operative when it is accepted in faith. Thus we do not baptise infants. There is, however, a practice in our churches of presenting young children at a service of public worship where the responsibilities of the parents and the church are recognised and prayers are offered for the parents and the child. Baptists believe that from birth all children are within the love and care of the heavenly Father and therefore within the operation of the saving grace of Christ; hence they have never been troubled by the distinction between baptised and unbaptised children. They have had a notable share with other groups of Christian people in service to children in Sunday schools, orphanages, education and child welfare.

We would claim that the baptism of believers by immersion is in accordance with and sets forth the central facts of the Gospel. It is an " acted creed." We value the symbolism of immersion following the Pauline teaching of the believer's participation in the death, burial and resurrection of our Lord (Romans vi. 3). As a matter of history, however, the recovery of the truth that baptism is only for believers preceded by some years the return by Baptists to the primitive mode of baptising by immersion, and it is a credible and responsible profession of faith on the part of the candidate for baptism which we hold to be essential to the rite. As a means of grace to the believer and to the church and as an act of obedience to our Lord's command, we treasure this sacrament. The New Testament clearly indicates a connection of the gift of the Holy Spirit with the experience of baptism which, without making the rite the necessary or inevitable channel of that gift, yet makes it the appropriate occasion of a new and deeper reception of it.

The Lord's Supper is celebrated regularly in our churches. The form of service, which is "congregational " and in which laymen have a part, preserves the New Testament conception of the Supper as an act of fellowship, a community meal. Yet as baptism is more than a dramatic representation of the facts of our redemption, so the Communion Service is more than a commemoration of the Last Supper and a showing forth " of the Lord's death until He come." Here the grace of God is offered and is received in faith; here the real presence of Christ is manifest in the joy and peace both of the believing soul and of the community; here we are in communion, not only with our fellow-members in the church, not only with the Church militant on earth and triumphant in heaven, but also with our risen and glorified Lord.

Membership of our local churches is normally consequent on Believers' Baptism, but differences of outlook and practice exist amongst us. "Close Membership" Baptist churches receive into their membership only those who have professed their faith in Christ by passing through the waters of baptism: "Open Membership" churches, though they consist, in the main, of baptised believers, receive also those Christians who profess such faith otherwise than in Believers' Baptism.

Similar differences are to be found amongst us on the question of those who may partake of the Lord's Supper. " Close Communion " churches invite to the Lord's table only those baptised on profession of faith. " Open Communion " churches welcome to the service all " who love the Lord Jesus Christ in sincerity." These differences do not prevent churches of different types from being in fellowship one with another nor from co-operating in the work of the Baptist Union, the Baptist Missionary Society and the Baptist World Alliance. They are united in the conviction that, in the New Testament teaching, personal faith in Christ is essential to the sacraments of the Gospel and the membership of the Church.

CHURCH AND STATE

(6) Our conviction of Christ's Lordship over His Church leads us to insist that churches formed by His

11

will must be free from all other rule in matters relating
to their spiritual life. Any form of control by the State
in these matters appears to us to challenge the " Crown
Rights of the Redeemer." We also hold that this freedom in Christ implies the right of the church to exercise
responsible self-government. This has been the Baptist
position since the seventeenth century, and it appears to
us the growth of the omnicompetent state and the threat
to liberty which has appeared in many parts of the world
today make more than ever necessary this witness to
spiritual freedom and responsibility which has always
been characteristic of the Baptist movement.

This freedom, however, has not led to irresponsibility
in our duties as citizens. We believe it is a Christian
obligation to honour and serve the State and to labour
for the well-being of all men and women. Baptists have
shared in many working-class movements, have a not
undistinguished record in social service, and were pioneers
in the modern missionary movement. They hold that
there is a responsibility laid upon each member of the
church and upon the churches themselves to apply their
faith to all the perplexities of contemporary life.

It will be seen that in this statement of the doctrine
of the Church the emphasis falls time and again upon the
central fact of evangelical experiences, that when God
offers His forgiveness, love and power the gift must be
personally accepted in faith by each individual. From
this follows the believer's endeavour to warlk in the way
of the Lord and to be obedient to His commandments.
From this follows, also, our traditional defence of civil
and religious liberty. It governs our conception of the
Church and our teaching on Believers' Baptism. Gratefully recognising the gifts bestowed by God upon other
communions, we offer these insights which He has
entrusted to us for the service of His whole Church.

Appendix E

SOME MODERN BOOKS ON THE NATURE OF THE CHURCH

Baptists thinking on the matters dealt with in these pages must take into careful account the results of the modern study of the New Testament and of the life of the primitive Church. It may be useful, therefore, to call attention to some of the more important books available in English. Bishop Lightfoot's *Dissertation on the Christian Ministry*, first published in 1868 as part of his commentary on *Philippians*, is "a standard classic" on its subject. Most modern treatment starts from its contention that what was originally a two-fold ministry (episcopoi—presbyters and deacons) became only later a three-fold ministry of bishops, presbyters and deacons. In 1881 Hatch published his *Organisation of the Early Christian Churches*, which sought to prove the Gentile origin of the term "bishop" as distinct from the Jewish term "presbyter"; the book excited considerable controversy, and its theory was adopted and developed by Harnack. R. W. Dale was able to invoke the authority of Lightfoot and Hatch for many of the views on Christian origins adopted in his *Manual of Congregational Principles*, published in 1884 by the Congregational Union. At about the same time the text of the *Didache* or *Teaching of the Twelve Apostles* was discovered and seemed to give clear evidence of the prophetic character of the earliest Christian ministry. The date and significance of the *Didache* have continued, however, down to the present day matters of keen discussion. In 1888 Gore attempted a "High Church" reply to Hatch and Harnack. His book, *The Church and the Ministry*, has had a very large circulation and has exerted a considerable influence on Anglican thought; in 1919, and again in 1936, it was revised and brought up-to-date by C. H. Turner. Gore argued that Christ instituted a visible society with a three-fold order of ministry and that " the apostolic succession must be reckoned as a permanent and essential element of Christianity." F. J. A. Hort's *The Christian Ecclesia* appeared in 1897; it is a sober and objective review of the New Testament evidence and has become a standard work. More recent scholars such as C. H. Dodd and R. Newton Flew confess their continued indebtedness to Hort. Also in 1897 there was published R. C. Moberly's *Ministerial Priesthood*, another " High Church " criticism of Lightfoot's thesis, which still has influence in certain circles. T. M. Lindsay's *The Church and Ministry in the Early Centuries*, 1902, is an interesting and competent survey of the whole field by an eminent Presbyterian scholar; it may still be recommended as one of the best books on the subject. C. H. Turner in " The Organisation of the Church," *Cambridge Medieval History*, Vol. I, 1911, and in *Studies in Early Church History*, 1912, and *Catholic and Apostolic*, 1931, maintained the general standpoint of Gore, as did the contributors to *Essays on the Early History of the Church and Ministry, edited by H. B. Swete*, 1918, and B. J. Kidd in his *History of the Church to 461*, 1921. On the other side we may note Gwatkin's *Early Church History*, 1909, which acknowledged its dependence on Lightfoot and Hort, various writings of J. Vernon Bartlet, including his 1924 Birkbeck Lectures, *Church-Life and Church-Order during the first Four Centuries*, 1943, John Oman's, *The Church and the Divine Order*, 1911, P. T. Forsyth's *The Church and the Sacraments*, 1917, C. Anderson Scott's *The Fellowship of the Spirit*, 1921, and *The Church, its Worship and Sacraments*, 1927, and P. Carnegie Simpson's, *The*

Evangelical Church Catholic, 1934. In 1929 the Anglican, B. H. Streeter, published *The Primitive Church,* which contends in candid, lively and provocative fashion for " a far greater diversity and variegation in Primitive Christianity than is commonly recognised." His views called forth various " High Church " protests, including *Episcopacy Ancient and Modern,* edited by Claude Jenkins and K. D. Mackenzie, 1930, but Streeter reasserted his main contentions in *The Cambridge Ancient History,* Vol. XI. 1936. More recent contributions from the " High Church " standpoint include A. M. Ramsey, *The Gospel and the Catholic Church,* 1936, important for its attempt to relate the nature and order of the Church to the death and resurrection of Jesus, L. S. Thornton *The Common Life in the Body of Christ,* 1942, and A. G. Hebert, *The Form of the Church,* 1944. From the " Free Church " standpoint R. Newton Flew's *Jesus and His Church,* 1938, is an important contribution; it is an elaborate and detailed argument, and has valuable references to the work of recent continental scholars such as Karl Holl, K. L. Schmidt and G. Gloege. Side by side with Flew's work may be set the recent study by a Scottish Presbyterian, George Johnston, *The Doctrine of the Church in the New Testament,* 1943, and, as a stimulating addition, D. T. Jenkins's *The Nature of Catholicity,* 1942. The composite volume which represents the report of the Theological Commission appointed by the Continuation Committee of the Faith and Order Movement, *The Ministry and the Sacraments,* edited by R. Dunkerley and A. C. Headlam, 1937, has in it much important material regarding the views of the different ecclesiastical traditions. T. S. Eliot's *The Idea of a Christian Society,* 1939, and John Baillie's *What is Christian Civilisation?* 2nd edition, 1947, raise a number of important contemporary issues. In 1946 there appeared under the editorship of K. E. Kirk, a volume of essays entitled *The*

Apostolic Ministry. The work of an able group of Anglo-Catholic scholars, it put forward the view that the episcopate is directly derived from the apostolate and is the essential ministry of the Church upon which all three forms of ministry depend. The main thesis of the book has called forth replies from within the Anglican Church (e.g. *The Ministry of the Church,* edited by Stephen Neill, 1947) and from those of other communions. T. W. Manson's *The Church's Ministry,* 1948, is a brief but weighty exposition from the Free Church standpoint. In 1950 there appeared an English translation by J. R. Coates of K. L. Schmidt's article on *The Church* in Kittel's *Theologisches Wörterbuch.* At the first Assembly of the World Council of Churches in Amsterdam in 1948 discussion took place on " The Universal Church in God's Design " (see Report, Vol. I), and in preparation for the Third World Conference on Faith and Order, Lund, 1952, a report on " The Church " and three volumes of confessional statements and biblical and theological essays are in preparation. D. T. Jenkins's *Tradition and the Spirit,* 1951, should also be noted, and also J. Robert Nelson's *The Realm of Redemption,* 1951, an able conspectus of discussions of the nature of the church in contemporary Protestant theology. It is clear that the debate of the last eighty years must be regarded as still inconclusive. It is equally clear, however, that the basic Free Church contention that Faith comes before Order, the Gospel before the Church, has not been invalidated.

INDEX